Overcoming Shame

Overcoming Shame

the hardest thing for people
to see is the way out

Marshall Chikaka

PARTRIDGE
A Penguin Random House Company

Print information available on the last page.

To order additional copies of this book, contact
Toll Free 800 101 2657 (Singapore)
Toll Free 1 800 81 7340 (Malaysia)
orders.singapore@partridgepublishing.com

www.partridgepublishing.com/singapore

CONTENTS

INTRODUCTION

Are you bound by shame? Are you covered in shame? Has it crept in your subconscious mind? Are you fighting feelings of worthlessness, insignificance and total loss or self-esteem? Are you struggling to wish away a sense of blowing it – big time or falling short of expectations as a husband a wife, a businessman, a spiritual leader or a believer? Are you having a difficult time to overcome the pain in your life, rejection the difficult situation you are in? In this book I am going to share timely thoughts that will help you break away from every tentacle of shame that has wrapped itself around your life and start enjoying your life as God intended you to, there is a way out!

Far too many believers are feeling dirty, worthless and ashamed of themselves. As a result, they feel unclean and therefore unworthy to approach God and have the living and intimate relationship that He wants to have with them! God wants you to experience His love for you and become your father and many even feel they are a mistake in life and that's the lie of the devil there is a tremendous difference between making a mistake and believing you are a mistake....if I don't see myself as being a mistake then it is I who must take responsibility and I am not ready to accept that I am a mistake no matter what's happening to me I know that there is a way out _ of this!

One of the things that I came to understand while I was going through a season of shame in my life is that the hardest thing for you to see during the difficult time is the way out!

As much as you can see the challenge but seeing the way out is difficult and the longer you experience a difficult time is the more you lose hope and the more you lose hope is the more you look to natural environment, external things the people around you, where you're born for solution and the problem is my external environment, the things around me does not line up with what God has for me you can't tell me who I am by where you find me, you can't tell me what I am capable to accomplish by just looking at me at a glimpse and some even blame others for being the cause of the difficulty they are experiencing, you must never blame anyone for being the cause of the difficulty you are experiencing because as long as you point at somebody else as the reason you're not moving, it means that you can't go forward until somebody comes back! There's a way out,

Henry David Thoreau said I quote "It's not what you look at that matters, it's what you see – what do you see? In the very heart of what you going through what do you see? this is what has propelled me to write this book to tell and encourage you that no matter what you are going through right now there is a way out,

Honestly speaking no one escapes some degree of trouble in their lives for it is so ever prevalent; it is the human experience, this realization does not mean we can't improve. It does mean we can accept our state of trouble lightens up on ourselves, have fun, and work on improving…we are a work in progress people see the difficult they are going through the shame that they are in but they don't see the way out, there is a way out.

My Prayer is that after reading this book you will let go and let God gently wash away every limitation of past obstacles and gradually transform you into the person you were created to become
You can Overcome "SHAME"

DEDICATION

"I have fought a good fight, I have finished my course,
I have kept the faith: 8: Henceforth there is laid up for me
a crown of righteousness, which the Lord, the righteous judge,
shall give me at that day: and not to me only, but unto all
them also that love his appearing– 2 Timothy 4: 7-8

This Book is dedicated to all those who one way or the other fell and still got up and limped their way to the finish line

It is such an inspiration to witness someone falling but still rising up and never giving up on their faith I salute and dedicate this book to such and may all those who are down find strength and courage to rise up again and not to focus on where they fell but focus on where they are rising to if they fell and got up You too can get up again because God is not finished with You

There's a way out!

A NOTE FROM MARSHALL

There's nothing more powerful than an idea whose time has come, for a long time always had a desire of writing a book and I believe it was not time yet, you can have an idea but if its not time its not a good idea and time comes by pain, time comes through hardships, through challenging situations. if you have never experienced any of that then you not ready for time, because its in time that God reveals Himself, so if you are going through any challenge hold on the time for your deliverance draws near, God is able to deliver you because of the pain that I experienced during the time of shame, out of that pain came this beautiful revelation that I am privileged to share in this book I thank my heavenly father for covering my shame, I came to understand during the time when I was down that "there's power that's found in Him that cannot be found in anything or anyone to lift you up when you down and that's God's power of love", I wouldn't be where I am without Him, His love is the reason I live, the reason I have confidence even in my downfall, the reason I am confident in my calling and purpose and the reason I breath and move, I will never trade where I am with Him for anything less than Him.

I thank God for this time He makes all things beautiful in its time; after going through a season of shame in my life based on the things that I will share later in this book, out of that shame came a certain level of glory that could not be revealed without going through what I experienced and this glory exposes itself only as you go through the challenging experiences I also came to understand that whatever I went through I say like the Apostle Paul "I would you should understand brethren, that things which happened to me have fallen out rather unto the furtherance of the gospel" so God had a reason for allowing me to go through the shame I went through and there was always strength in every stage I found myself in; that's proof to me that God was always involved so by His mercy, grace and love I wrote this book that I believe will help and encourage you to rise and become that which God wants you to become despite of what you going through and never let those who don't know your purpose, timing nor placement determine your value and relevance always know that there is a way out

ACKNOWLEDGEMENTS

For over ten years people have been building into my life. Books by authors I never met and tapes by people I never knew have contributed to my growth in Christ, I'm so grateful for all the teachers I have had over the years. I am sure each one has contributed something to this book Pastor Jimmy Crompton of Word of Faith Christian center, Jason Bowen my Bible School Dean, Reverend Jared Graham and his family for playing such an important role in my life, they believed in my calling and they nurtured it in every way you can possibly think of, Pastor Nyaniso Zumani my good friend who was there for me and was used by God to open doors of opportunity for me, Mr Washington and Mrs. Orienda Sabelo who recently went home to be with the Lord will always think of her and thank you so much for adopting and providing for all my needs during my staying in your home and I want to thank High Praise Centre and its leadership they are the last of a dying breed, where relationships count most, Bishop Benjamin Dube for believing in me and inspiring my life of ministry would never trade my fellowship and relationship with him for anything. Pastor Bonisani Dube for identifying my gift, supporting, mentoring and encouraging me and because of his words "that in order for me to be what God wants me to be I have to keep doing what God told me to do then its in continuing that I will become what God wants me to be" I believe I am still pressing on despite of what I face because I live by those words and the bottom line is ministry and integrity.

I also want to thank Leslie Ngobeni and his family for believing in me and always encouraging me every time that I felt like giving up they were to me what I couldn't be for myself they had this gift of bringing the best of me at all times and I also want to thank my dear friends Portia Chauke and Joseph Simukai for being always there for me motivating and pushing me towards Greatness and I want to thank my family especially my dear precious mother Rachel who loved me unconditionally thank you so much for being the greatest mum in the whole world., your prayers made me what I am

And last but not least I want to thank all my enemies without them the table of the Lord wouldn't be laid

CHAPTER ONE

What is Shame?

*…"Shame is so real and its effects are devastating sometimes
we don't realize that what we struggling with is shame"*

Do not fear, for you will not be neither be disgraced, for you will not
be put to SHAME; for you will forget the SHAME of your youth, and will
not remember the reproach of your widowhood anymore. For your maker is
your husband the Lord of hosts is His name and your redeemer is the Holy
one of Israel; He is called the God of the whole earth _Isaiah 54:4

We live in an atmosphere of shame. Somebody somewhere is ashamed
of something. We are ashamed of everything that is real about us; ashamed
of ourselves, of our relatives, our families, our incomes, our accents, our
citizenships, our skin color, our challenges, our societies, our opinions, and
even our experiences, in this chapter we going to look at what Shame is and
how to easily identify it in your life.

According to the dictionary shame is a painful emotion caused by
consciousness of guilt, short coming or impropriety that degenerates to
demeaning disgrace or disrepute. It is a negative emotion that combines
feelings of dishonor, unworthiness and ignomy. For instance when you
do something wrong, you feel guilty and ashamed especially if your
wrong doing spills over to the public, many people can handle shame
as long as their secret remains known only to them, but the moment
all is out in the public and on everybody's lips they can't stand the

humiliation, the embarrassment, the condemnation and yes the shame involved,

Imagine the woman who was caught in the act of adultery in John chapter 8 it was all good as long as her story was private but the moment her story was public it was another thing.

I remember my story of shame that I will later on share with you, as long as nobody knew about what had happened, I was able to deal with the shame that was only known to me but the moment everybody knew, it was a different story after all, and that's the basis of shame it's really not some personal mistake of ours, but the ignominy, the humiliation we feel that we must be what we are without any choice in the matter, and that this humiliation is seen by everyone

I like what Blake Edwards said about shame he said "shame is an unhappy emotion invented by pietists in order to exploit the human race" and its very true that's all shame does its an un happy emotion, shame can also be a result of something terribly painful inflicted on us by someone else, the person might be a relative or a close family member or someone we had trusted so much this could be through molestation, abuse, rape, demeaning words or general treatment many people do struggle with this kind of shame some live in denial, while others isolates themselves and withdraw from people because they can't trust anybody and this kind of shame is what is holding people hostage

"Shame is so real and its effects are devastating sometimes we don't realize that what we struggling with is shame"

Our Journey as Christians is full of challenges and one of the greatest challenge we face is when a constant barrage of the question "will I ever shake off the feeling of my disgraceful past?" this lingers or keeps popping up in our subconscious mind when your conscious is constantly bombarded with nasty, painful and shameful thoughts of your past that you seek to forget, when your shameful past is constantly thrown right in your face either by the accuser of the brethren or by your fellow brother or sister, like the Pharisees in the book of John 8 who kept accusing the woman caught in adultery as they kept asking Jesus what should be done to her and you will definitely find yourself contending secretly with Shame.

All of us we have a past that we would gladly love to forget, it is sad that many people remain locked up in their past allowing every bit of it to not only haunt them and limit them but also to deter them from enjoying their glorious present as a matter of fact, the answer to the above question reveals the unseen warfare we wage on Shame, precisely it depicts how many believers wrestle disgraceful acts, past dishonestly and unmentionable past experience that keep flushing in their minds at the least expected time such as during the worship service or when one is alone. These ignominies that endlessly nag us when we want to move ahead cause us to doubt if at all any genuine and significant change did really took place in our hearts when we got saved. But I have good news for you the devil is a liar you can overcome shame

Shame is really deeply rooted in the wrong that we did, it is also embedded in the experiences we went through whether willingly or unwillingly. For instance when one engages in sexual promiscuity it can cause them to be ashamed afterwards just as much as someone else who goes through sexual molestation by a stranger or a close relative and when a person experiences shame, they feel there is something basically wrong with them, so they blame themselves for having allowed that particular thing to happen to them, some resort to punishing themselves in a bid to pay for what they did at the end of the day they feel worse because that only aggravates the situation.

Shame is so real and its effects are devastating sometimes we don't realize that what we struggling with is shame. I decided to write the following questions just to help you determine if you are struggling with shame or not

1: Do you often meditate on your past failures or experiences of rejection?
2: are there certain things about your past which you cannot recall without experiencing strong, painful, shameful emotions?
3: Do you feel bad after repeating mistakes over and over again?
4: are you disgusted with yourself?
5: Do you feel unworthy or inferior?

6: Are you struggling with self-acceptance?

7: Do you feel like you can't recover from a terrible, nasty past?

8: Do you think you are a total failure?

These are just but a few questions that can serve as an eye-opener for anyone struggling with shame. in this book; I will help you in details, some of these issues and help you get a solution to deal with them. Remember that God is still able to deliver you from shame no matter how deep it has taken root in your life. His blood is still powerful to erase every trace of shame haunting you and eroding your self-esteem.

He is able to revoke every stench of shame from your past, repair your damaged self-esteem and clothe you with dignity again remember Isaiah 54:4 the Bible says that "Do not fear, for you will not be neither be disgraced, for you will not be put to SHAME; for you will forget the SHAME of your youth, and will not remember the reproach of your widowhood anymore. For your maker is your husband the Lord of hosts is His name and your redeemer is the Holy one of Israel; He is called the God of the whole earth" halleluiah your maker is your husband the Lord of host He will cover you and you will not remember the reproach of your widowhood. the Apostle Paul said in Philippians 1:12 he said *"But I would you should understand brethren, that the things which happened to me have fallen out rather unto the furtherance of the gospel* "in other words the things that happened to him happened not to destroy him, not to kill him, not to embarrass him and not to steal from him but to equip him so he may have an ability and the grace to further the gospel and that's the heart of the father that lives may be touched. I believe out of the shame I experienced came this powerful book that will bless, touch and transform people who are going through what I went through and more and that's the essence of this book to help you overcome and break away from the clutches of shame and start enjoying your life as God intended and designed it to be despite of what's happening in your life or what has happened, what you did or what you did not do because the things that happened to you have fallen rather unto the furtherance of the gospel", We run with what God has said about us, not what the circumstances are saying", not what people are saying to you or what you are saying about yourself we were created to do great and be great and not to fold our gifts as a dog folds its tail, No we are not the tail but we are the head no matter what has happened to you Your maker is your husband (My God) He will cover you whenever there is no one to cover you some of you as you reading this book you feel naked I have good news for you God wants to cover your nakedness, without asking anyone's permission, He wants to bless you, He wants to use you to further the Gospel and even if He has to use shame to do that, You can overcome shame

CHAPTER TWO

My story of Shame

"Shame used to run my life, out of a need to constantly prove myself"

Our stories are not meant for everyone, hearing them is a privilege, and we should always ask ourselves this before we share; "who has earned the right to hear my story?" if we have one or two people in our lives who can sit with us and hold space for our shame stories, and love us for our strengths and struggles, we are incredibly blessed. If we have a friend, or a small group of friends, or family who embraces our imperfections, vulnerabilities, and power, and fills us with a sense of belonging, we are truly blessed. If we can share our story with someone who responds with empathy and understanding, shame can't survive and at the same time shame derives its power from being unspeakable. I trust that by sharing and speaking my story of shame everyone reading this will embrace my imperfections and not only mine but others as well and that will disempower shame

Growing up in an abused family and struggled to feel good about myself in the wider world, especially in school. I was often blamed for things that went wrong both big and small, and over time I was convinced that there was something inherently wrong with me. I covered up my deep feelings of unworthiness by striving to be a perfect student "I was always trying to find a way to stand out as intelligent, I was always the first to raise my hand in class that was more like my life in school and outside school I scrambled to avoid scrutiny. I was withdrawn, never inviting my classmates and friends to our chaotic home. I felt ashamed, isolated and uneasy

In High School, I hustled for academic attention, paired with my deep desire to hide the other aspects of my life, our family was an averaged family four boys and one girl, and growing up in this family was very difficult because we used to witness my father abusing our precious mother in front of us and sometimes in the public where the whole neighborhood would come out awaken by the noise of my mother screaming and everyone would watch helplessly as my father would beat her and no one would do anything about it and this was a terrible and a worst thing for me, I always asked myself why this was happening in front of people and more over my friends how was I going to face them tomorrow? I could handle the shame as long as they fought in private but the moment they fought in public it was something else the shame that I would experience especially in the morning I was even embarrassed to go to the shops because everyone is looking at you and talking about your family and the thought of that shame really destroyed my childhood cause here is a thing about Shame: it binds you, enslaves you, restricts you, I was not able to do the other activities that other young people would do that shame limits you and robs you of the capacity to either imagine or to act.

You might be asking yourself why I have to mention my Past. Because the past does play a part in our future and some of the things that we go through are as a result of our upbringing so in order to deal with the now we have to look back in the past it will all make sense to you as I explain my story of shame you will be able to understand my story of shame after understanding my past so just be patient with me as I take you back. my father being the abuser he was to my mother and sometimes to us, he was a very strict man so I found myself living a life of performance in order for him to accept me and he also created this mind in us of how worthless woman were so I grew up with that belief that woman were worthless we as man were supposed to treat them as nothing and as you going to follow my story you going to see how that really affected me now, how it all connected itself with the story of my shame. And I want you to understand that I don't blame anyone for what my past did because I have a choice whether my past can affect me or not because I have a future to live no matter what has happened in your past remember there is a future

Bless her heart my mother who was a very committed Christian woman who was serving God with all her heart and she never realized that the things that she had to suffer then, they will be rewarded in the future and also further the gospel. our house was almost like a church because of the woman gathering every time in prayer believing that if they can pray more then my father would stop his abusive ways but the most strange of all things I never understood growing up as a young man was what was going on because the more they prayed is actually the more my father would become worse, shame actually makes believing the gospel impossible and forces us into patterns of behavior that are decidedly un-Christ like imagine having attitude towards the praying woman? But it never stopped them they continued praying to a point where I told my mother that she should stop praying maybe all can be normal but she continued in what she was doing she never gave up to a point where I was so convinced in what she was doing, it was not necessary the prayers that changed me it was her perseverance that really moved me despite of what she was going through in her life but still she kept her faith in the God that never changes to me that was the highest form of sacrifice to be done, going through pain and still holding on and continue believing and trusting your God that to me became a planted seed in my life to a point where I gave my life to Christ because of her suffering.

That's why it's so important for us to understand that what we go through in our personal lives we actually going through it for other people it's not about us and it's not personal as well God is in control always pray and ask God especially when you going through pain and difficulties ask Him what He is doing and cooperate with Him He is a loving God He knows the plans that He has for us and those plans are not to harm us or destroy us but to give us hope and future after giving my life to Christ there was a drastically change in my life it was more like my life was now supernatural I was on fire for God as young as I was then I started feeling the urge and the call of God upon my life that I decided to go to Bible School but my father was so much against that and was so much convinced that I was throwing and wasting my life by enrolling to a theological school and I wanted to prove him wrong, that's the greatest mistake we do we want to prove God to people but God doesn't want us to prove Him, He can prove Himself. All God wants from us is to reflect Him and He has the ability to prove Himself so on the other side my father wanted to prove to us that this thing of Christianity does not work so we found ourselves in a battle of trying to prove to each other and it happened as time progressed and was maturing in the things of God I was led by the spirit to come to South Africa in 2000 after my conversion in 1999 and enroll in a theological school and I obeyed the voice I came to South Africa and to me it was two things following my calling and running away from my father in order to prove to him that the road that I had chosen was the true road and not the road that he wanted us to take that is the ancestral road and he was so convinced that the Christianity road was a waste of time and we would never make it in life as long as we walk in that Christian road and not with him and to me it was not true.

When I came to South Africa life was not easy it was even more tougher than it was before and now I can understand why life became tougher its all because now I had discovered my purpose and I was pursuing it the enemy doesn't have a problem with you as long as you not moving the moment you start moving he has a problem now I had so much pressure in me trying to prove to my father that Christianity was the road I did all I could in my strength to hide all that I was going through from my father so that his point won't be valid; this became sort of like a game that I started playing and life is not a game neither is Christianity, we have to refuse to be ignorant and face the challenges that we face with faith in our hearts that God is control despite of what we face. Even if its witnessed by others because its in them witnessing that they will see God in me when I refuse to give up I continued playing the game of trying to please man instead of trying to please God because the truth is when you please God then you don't have to please man even though I had nothing to my name materially I did all I could to get the best things so as to prove to Him that being in the Ministry was not a mistake that I did. So shame was actually running my life, out of a need to constantly prove myself, I was always under pressure in trying to prove to him that Christianity was the way. Sometimes it's not in proving that Christianity works because of material things, but most of the time the most effective way to communicate that Christianity is real is when you go through suffering and you continue holding on in that suffering and never give up that people will see God and that's exactly what happened to me in my years of growing up when I saw the perseverance of my mother that moved me, when they see you go through rough times but still holding on that is what moves people, in my game of proving God opened a door for me to serve under the leadership of Bishop Benjamin Dube and to me that was a blessing to be privileged to be even acquainted with him is one of the greatest honors in my life to experience personal fellowship, relationship and mentorship to me is amazing I thank God for the great man of God and his brother Pastor Bonisani for mentoring and giving direction and meaning to my life of ministry and after having met these great people I thought my life was now where I wanted it to be, I broke the news to my family back home that I am working with Bishop Benjamin Dube and to me it was a way of trying to put a point across that now what was I telling you about ministry is real, but it was not all I had in mind the pressure became even more I had to consistently live up to that high standard of the circle of people and influence that was around me trying to fit in their world not knowing that time was set by God and as time progressed involved with these great names there was an expectation from my father to do big things for him because now that I am acquainted to these great man, man that have names all over the world and that I believed he even doubted whether it was true but nonetheless he had such expectations the expectations were made obvious in some of our phone conversations that we made he would ask how much I was earning, what property I had and was I planning to buy him a house and all that and what this did to me was put more pressure for performance I would constantly lie to him by mentioning big amounts of money as the salary I was earning so as to prove my point.

I remember the first time going to the Bishop's house and taking pictures of his pictures on the wall and I called my family telling them that I am sitting with Bishop Benjamin Dube in his home this was a breakthrough, this was amazing this was all good but what I was failing to understand was the time factor that even though I was in the presence of great but if its not my time yet then its not my time, God makes all things beautiful in its time then God graced me I was ordained to be a Pastor it was the best day of my life finally my dream had come to pass that's what I came to South Africa for what an accomplishment it was when I broke the news to my family the whole family including relatives all were in Awe of what

God can do taking a Young insignificant boy making him meet and be acquainted to such names and getting ordained to be a pastor under such names it was a dream coming true God was so good at High Praise Centre the calling and gift I had in my life started to become so evident as God started using me at the level where I was I had such influence in the lives of people, they looked up to me as a role model especially in the youth God was using me big time I had all the attention I wanted but that is what got me into trouble I started making friends with the wrong people the power of association and having those kind of friends I started finding myself in unfamiliar places but because of compromise sometimes we don't rebuke what is wrong so as to please and keep our friends, I came to learn that whatever you cannot confront you can never overcome so I found myself in the place that I couldn't confront the place called "the place of trading"

The place of trading

The place of trading is a place where because of lack of discipline and disobedience you find yourself in that place and in this place even though you're born again and loves God but the presence of the Lord will not be there: when I say the presence of the Lord I am not talking about God being in the place physically but I am taking about His purpose prevailing in your life. You remember the bible says in Genesis 3:8 that they heard the voice of the Lord God walking in the garden in the cool of the day: and Adam and his wife hid themselves from the presence of the Lord God amongst the trees of the garden? they couldn't hide from His presence because God is omnipresence what they were hiding from was God purpose for their lives God had intended them not to eat of the fruit of the garden but to obey Him and walk according to His purpose and plan for them but they disobeyed and when they disobeyed they went out of the presence of God, in other words they went out of the purpose of God and you remember Genesis 4:16 and Cain went out from the presence of the Lord, and dwelt in the land of Nod, on the east of Eden that doesn't mean where Cain went God was not there it means when Cain disobeyed and went to the land of Nod God's purpose was not there God's purpose was in the place God wanted Cain to be that's the place of obedience, obeying His plan and purpose for your life where He wants you to be.: You remember the familiar story that was always being taught in the Sunday school the story of Jonah and the big fish? I want to show you something in that story and I pray that its familiarity wouldn't rob you of what God wants to say to you God wanted Jonah to go to Nineveh but Jonah disobeyed God and went to Tarshish instead of going to Nineveh and Tarshish is very interesting place according to the historical geographical set up of the place it was a trading place, in other words it was a place where people would come from different cities and meet up and trade what they had so Tarshish was a place of trading, you trade your abilities, You trade your life for death, you trade your gift, you trade your destiny, you trade your calling, you trade the anointing, you trade the responsibility God gave you, you trade your integrity, you trade your reputation, and you trade your obedience for something less its in this place that the enemy gives you an apple and takes away your destiny, when I talk about the enemy I am not just referring to Satan but I am taking about anyone or anything that takes you away from God is your enemy in my case woman became my enemy. I found myself in the place of trading God had purposed me to go to Nineveh and instead I went to Tarshish I found myself in a ship headed to Tarshish surrounded by woman and these woman would actually buy me gifts and even though in my spirit I knew that God was not sending me in the place I continued in my disobedience brothers and sisters always remember that when you disobey God there's always a price to pay the bible says Jonah paid the fare and boarded the ship that was going to Tarshish where he was going to trade the responsibilities that God had given him concerning Nineveh, he was going to trade the anointing upon his life, he was going to trade honor, the honor of God appointing you to be His vessel now while he was in the ship God sends a great wind and the ship was threatening to sink its so strange that sometimes even in your disobedience God will send all kinds of warning just to remind you that where you are is not the place that you suppose to be but even though there was a great wind Jonah was in the bottom deck of the ship sleeping in other words he was so comfortable in the ship sometimes we get comfortable in our sins and we tell our selves that I am used to this so its okay I would still fulfill my Pastoral duties and yet living in sin and nobody knew that and that was my comfort zone but its amazing that while he was sleeping the mariners came and woke him up telling him the same thing that God told him to Arise they said Arise and call on your god maybe he can hear you the ship is sinking but they realized later that he was the cause so he requested to be thrown in the water where the fish came and swallowed him God is so faithful that even in your sin He will still protect and cover you so that when you come to your senses then you can obey what He has called you to so the wind actually was a tool that God used to expose Jonah in him comfort zone of disobedience

The place of exposing

The exposing place is a place where God will send a great wind upon the sea, and there will be a mighty tempest on the sea and the ship will threaten to break up, in your sin there is a moment where all hell will break loose, in other words your sin will find you, the bible says Jonah after he paid the fare to go to Nineveh God sent a great wind and the ship was almost breaking I enjoyed my sin knowing that nobody was seeing me but it was just a matter of time when I was exposed and the reason God exposes us is not so he can embarrass or humiliate us no, I like what Pastor Moody said "God exposes us at times because we become too comfortable in our dysfunctional place" the bible says in Acts 12: Peter was in Jail and the angel came and did something strange the bible says the angel hits Peter and that hitting was affliction; this is strange because if you think why would God inflict pain on his servants, on those He love?, this is interesting because the angel strikes people why? Because Peter is not just in prison he's also in chains, he is already confined to a small place, but on top of all that his movement is restricted and so on his right and on his left his chained to soldiers that are guarding him so his life is confined and on top of that he's chained to people who's responsibility is to keep him in that state and all of this is happening on the night before he's getting ready to go to trial and ultimately be executed so everything around him is designed to restrict his movement, to keep him in that state long enough until they can ultimately kill him, so God intervenes and exposes you and in exposing you he's actually protecting you from being killed and watch this in the midst of all this Peter had the nerve to go and sleep and so the angel hits him, why? Because Peter has got to way comfortable in a dysfunctional situation when you get to comfortable in your sin God will expose you, can I tell you the uncomfortable truth?, the uncomfortable truth is sometimes God will hurt you to promote you, sometimes God will demote you to elevate you, because God is looking at your life and He says "you got way to comfortable in a dysfunctional situation", some of you its exactly where your life is right now, the reason things are crumbling around you, the reason why things are not going the way you want them to is because God is saying you got to comfortable in a dysfunctional situation and its time for me to expose you, you not suppose to stay in that place, you remember Elijah God sends him to the brook saying I have commanded the ravens to feed you and Elijah goes to the brook, imagine he's going where God sends him, but watch this! the ravens feeds him at the brook!, he had water at the brook!, bread and meat at the brook!, but then after a while the bible says the brook dries up wait a minute you mean you send me to a place, I did what you wanted me to do, and you dried the brook? Why would God bring me to the brook and dry the brook up? And God says because I allowed it because you got to comfortable because the only thing you could eat at the brook was what the ravens were bringing you and what they could only fit in their mouth and God said I had to dry the brook up because it was not my will for you to live the rest of your life on scraps, I was to comfortable in depending on the woman who were providing me with material things and the thing about it is they were not just providing; I was paying a price for that and as time progressed in my comfort ability God had to expose me and all that I was doing was known by my leaders and in front of the whole congregation I was suspended of all my pastoral duties and my story was out in the public and shame took its course in my life I had to face people and deal with the shame it was an embarrassing moment of my life

Shame is always easy to handle if you have someone to share it with and to this point I never had anyone to share it with because of the fear of rejection I kept my story to myself so that I can fit in with others, I tried all I could to hide from people that's why I started to isolate myself and the thing is we cannot grow when we are in shame.

But having gone through all that I went through the shame and everything connected to it and I am here to tell you that it was not an easy road it was a painful road but thanks be to God who always gives us the victory I am here to tell you that even if you going through shame, hurt, disappointment or whatever I want you to know that there is a way out of this all you have to do is STAND because there is a way out

The place of death

The place of death is a place you come into still performing but dead, still used of God but dead, still preaching but dead, still leading worship but dead, still doing everything required to do as a service to God but still dead there is a scripture in the book of Exodus that caught my attention Exodus 28 I kept reading it over and over and over and seemed though the Holy spirit was saying something to me, in Exodus 28:42-43 it says "and thou shalt make them linen breeches to cover their nakedness from the loins even unto the thighs shall they reach and they shall be upon Aaron and upon his sons, when they came in unto the tabernacle of the congregation and when they came near unto me to minister at the alter in the holy place, listen to this that they bare not iniquity and die it shall be a statute forever unto him and his seed after him, I want you to notice a couple of things first of all God said I want Aaron when he comes to the holy place, into the holy of holies I want, him to come in and outwardly he will have a religious robe on, he will look the part outwardly, but he said you tell him that when he comes into my presence he needs to have linen breeches on that will cover his waist down to his thighs and his loins what he was talking about is the underwear, now listen to what He is saying He's saying when that priest on the day of atonement comes in and he stands by the ark of the covenant where God's holy presence dwelled it was there where God says my glory will be this will be the God box on planet earth and I will live in there until my son Jesus comes and He said you tell Aaron the high Priest to come in and when he comes in he's going to look religious, he will have the breast plate, he will have the robe, he will look like a Christian, but he said tell him to make sure he has his underclothes on, because if he doesn't have his underwear clothes he will die when he gets into my presence and listen to this he said this shall be established as a law from generations to generations in other words no matter what happens in time this will never change that when people try to come into my presence without wearing their underclothes they will surely die, God doesn't just want us to look religious on the outside He doesn't want us just to come to church on Sunday and worship and praise and people look at you and say man they really have a walk with God, people will see what you have on the outside but God will see what's going on in your private life when He says keep your linen breeches what He was talking about is sexual purity and notice the only one who whether or not he had his underclothes on was Aaron and God everybody else thought he looked like a Christian, you see the devil was a church kid Satan was in heaven the bible says he looked like a Christian on the outside but the issue is what's going on in your private life and God says if you want to live you have to keep your underclothes on and if you don't my presence will die in your life, the anointing will die in your life, praise will die in your life, you will come to church and get in His presence and not even feel Him because outwardly you saying I am Christian but your private life is not pure. I would come in God's presence and people would admire me preaching but what they didn't know was what was going on in my private life many people are ministering before God and they look okay on the outside but inside they dead you might be reading this and for years you have been ministering to God without your underclothes I am here to tell you that its time for you to stand up and come against sexual sins

The Place of standing up

Ladies and gentleman there are three things that I want to draw your attention to three things that the angel did when he came to Peter while he was in prison and in chains the bible says in Acts 12 the Angel shine light in the cell that's revelation and the angel hits Peter that's affliction and the third thing the angel did was he said "STAND UP" and that's resurrection I am here to tell you that you have to stand and the amazing thing is the two things the angel did for him, the angel shone the light for him and the angel hit him but the third thing Peter had to do for himself the angel said Stand up, in other words the angel was saying Peter I know you in prison but stand up, Peter I know you are in chains but stand up, I know you in a messed up situation Peter but stand up, I Know you going through divorce, but stand up, I know you have to deal with the sickness, but stand up, I know you didn't do anything to deserve this but stand up, I know you going through shame but stand up, I just fill like telling somebody to stand up, I don't care what it is stand up to it, I know they left you, I know they accusing you, I know they talking about you, but stand up to it, when the angel said to Peter stand up he was saying I don't care what it is, I don't care how many times you fall, I don't care how difficult it is, stand up

You remember the story in Genesis 21 after when Hagar and Ishmael were kicked out of Abraham's home the bible says that Abraham only gives Hagar and Ishmael a little bit of food and a little bit of water in a jar and they were kicked out of the house then the Hagar takes the baby Ishmael into the desert and around verse 16 it says they ran out of water and they ran out of food and so Hagar couldn't STAND to watch her baby die of hunger in her hands so the bible says she puts Ishmael under the bush and goes a distance turns away and sits down waits for the baby to die and verse 18 says when God speaks up one of the first things that God says to Hagar is STAND UP God was kind of asking was it right what Sarah did? No, was it right that Abraham kicked you out No, was the divorce fair? No, did you do anything for them to betray you? No, did you deserve to do all the work and not get a promotion? No, but when God speaks what does He says? STAND UP now watch this verse 19 says when Hagar stands up she sees a well of water the water had been there the whole time but she never would have seen it if she didn't STAND, I am here to tell someone that this is not your season to die, this is not your season to quit, there's joy, there's peace, there's breakthrough, there's provision in the name of Jesus but you not going to see it if you not going to STAND UP and the bible says when Peter stood up the moment when Peter stood up the chains began to fall, I don't care what you going through but when you STAND UP, chains of depression, chains of despair, chains of shame will begin to fall now watch this story when Peter stood up and the chains fell then the angel said put on your sandals and garment I don't have time to talk about the garment and shoes but what I want you to see is that Peter the whole time that he was in prison he had the keys, don't you remember when Jesus thou art Peter and on this rock I build my church Peter had the key all this time Halleluiah its time to STAND UP you got the key

CHAPTER THREE

My side of Story

"Tell us then, what you think?" – Matthew 22:17a ESV

Our stories are not meant for everyone. Hearing them is a privilege, and we should always ask ourselves this before we share: "who has earned the right to hear my story?" if we have one or two people in our lives who can sit with us and hold space for our shame stories, and love us for our strengths and struggles, we are incredibly blessed. If we have a friend or small group of friends, or family who embraces our imperfections, vulnerabilities, and power, and fills us with a sense of belonging, we are truly blessed, but it's not everyone who is meant to hear our stories, not everyone who seems to be concerned is concerned and not everyone who seems to care does care

In the absence of truth you can never defeat the devil after this is the motto that I am living with at the present moment because after my suspension in the church and my story of Shame was out on the open many people still wanted to know from my side what really happened they wanted to know my side of story. Every time I met someone who was aware or has heard about my story the first thing they would say is **"tell us then, what you think"** I believe part of the reason why they would ask is because they wanted to hear my side of story, as the saying goes "there's always two sides of a story" so people wanted to hear what really happened from my side they heard from the side of the church now they wanted to hear from the horse's mouth and so that's why I decided to write this chapter to tell my side of story in my opening this chapter I made a statement that I want to repeat again that is we have to understand that "in the absence of truth you can never defeat the devil, people say there are two sides of a story, that is his side and her side in the case of a couple maybe going through a divorce or having some challenges and all but I like what Bishop Tudor Bismarck said he said "there are five sides to every story, not two sides and that is his side, her side, the perceived side, the truth and God's side. Now I am sure you want to know my answer to all the people that were questioning me? Now let's look at a certain story in the book of Matthew 22:17

The Bible tells a powerful story of the Herodias after being sent by the Pharisees posed this question to Jesus saying "tell us then, what you think is it lawful to pay taxes to Caesar or not? So they came to Jesus and said "tell us then, what do you think? Is it lawful to pay taxes to Caesar or not? But notice this in verse 15 the bible says even though it was a good question but the reason they asked it was that they might entangle him in his talk, what we need to understand brethren is that the enemy is not after your story but the enemy is after what you going to say about your story because whatever you say will set a course in your life by what you say so the enemy will question you so as to trap you, sometimes people can put pressure on you and if you are not careful you going to say things that later on will work against you or regret, so its important to always be careful of what you say so it was not about the question but it was about the answer cause the Pharisees understood the power of the tongue that whatever Jesus would say would actually set the course of his life, now Jesus aware of their malice said "why put me to the test, you hypocrites? Show me the coin for the tax and they brought him a denarius and Jesus said to them "whose image and likeness is this? And they said Caesar's then he said to them therefore render to Caesar's the things that are Caesar's and to God the things that are God's" in other words you have to render to God what belongs to God and to Caesar what belongs to Caesar what he was simply saying was the truth is, even though you see two sides of a coin but the truth will always be the truth many in those days didn't want to pay taxes to Caesar because he was abusing their tax money but still Jesus wanted them to understand that the truth remains even though Caesar was abusing the tax but the truth was what prevailed that's paying your tax. The problem that we have as a people is we always want to blame others so we may make ourselves look good in a shameful situation but I want you to know that you must never try to defend yourself in whatever situation you may find yourself in even if you are wronged or you have wronged its not your part to defend yourself because the moment you do so, then God seizes to be your defender, my God let me say that again Never try to defend yourself because when you do so then God seizes to be your defender always tell the truth and the truth will set you free but we hide our shame, we cover it up by making excuses and blaming others for where we find ourselves I had all the reason to be angry with the people who exposed me but I had to make a choice whether to answer the people who were asking my side of story by telling them how evil those people were or by telling the truth of what happened and take full responsibility of my actions and all I did say to all the people who were asking me was the truth I want to submit this to you brethren that we don't like to take responsibility because we live in a victimization culture look at this you remember the prodigal son? The devil didn't spend his money, no con- artist tricked him, he was not a victim of a scheme, but he is the reflection of the absence of discipline. I feel like telling someone that I needed a moment to think, it was not the ladies that I sinned with their fault, it was not the people who exposed me fault it was my fault I was so ignorant because of my loneliness I lowered my standards I knew that these women were not for me, I knew that God had something else for me but I kept forcing myself on something that didn't line up with His will, and that's what got me into trouble I want to tell somebody that I had to tell the truth about my side and the truth is it was not anybody's fault it was my fault the absence of discipline many people find themselves into trouble and most of the time is because of lack of discipline God wants the best from us its not that He wants us not to enjoy, but He knows what's good for us, but the good news is that even if you find yourself in trouble Psalms 34:6 says "this poor man cried, the Lord heard him and delivered him out of all his troubles" in other words he got himself into trouble but still God delivered him out of them all so when they said "tell us then what you think?, I said to them "lack of discipline got me here"

CHAPTER FOUR

The road of Shame

"And when he had spent all, there arose a mighty famine in that land; and he began to be in want! - Luke 15:14

The road is shame is the road that you have to begin to walk after your sin has been exposed and everybody knows about it and now you have to face people, the road of shame is the road that you have to walk after discovering that the you are in a shameful situation the prodigal son after he had spent all he had a road to walk and God allows you to walk in that road not to embarrass or humiliate you but He allows you to walk in that road because before you can get the signet ring, the fatted calf you have to walk in that road and the reason you have to walk in that road is because its in the road that you are made so that you may qualify to get the ring and the seal of approval the prodigal son everything that was going to make him qualify for approval was in that road as a matter of fact the most valuable route was not the one when he had money it was the route going home with nothing and its in that road that God makes you, changes your character, changes the way you think, the way you act, and changes your thinking

It was a road of shame

"And he went and joined himself to a citizen of that country; and he sent him into his fields to feed swine! - Luke 15: 15

It was a road of shame because he was in shame of living a life that is beyond him, living a low life and yet this young man was a Jew and his father was a rich man but now he found himself working with pigs things that are beyond his covenant and he's forced to do so because he was disobedient to his gift and he was in the road of shame because he couldn't manage what his father gave him so he was experiencing shame even though he thought of going back home but shame was all around him, shame that he was lost all that he demanded from his father and as a matter of fact for a young man like him to ask his father's inheritance while the father was still alive it was considered to be disgraceful it was like the son was wishing his father to die, now he found himself working with pigs that was shameful because of who he was, the shame of not having anyone giving you food but having to eat with the swine that was shameful

It was a road of thought

"And when he came to himself, he said, how many hired servants of my father have bread enough and to spare, and I perish with hunger! – Luke 15:17

I recently read an article about prisoners how they believe in order for a prisoner to be transformed they needed isolation that could give them a season for atonement, introspection and meditation it was there belief that much of the crimes committed was at the hands of those who don't practice thinking. So people who broke the law, people who found themselves in trouble when they got caught, when they stood before the magistrate asked themselves what was I thinking?; I remember sitting in the church office surrounded by my leaders after I was caught in my sin the first thing in my mind was the question what was I thinking? Ladies and gentlemen I don't know how many of you have had that moment where you find yourself in something and asked yourself, what was I thinking?, how in the world did I do something that silly, how in the world did I not see that coming, I know better than this, what was I thinking, one of the revelations the Holy Spirit gave me was that the enemy tries to keep you so busy so you don't have time to think, we as Christians we do everything, we worship, we praise but we don't practice meditation, we do very little introspection, very little thinking so much so that when church gets quiet we think something is wrong, in the road of thought they may take everything away from you, they may embarrass you, they may leave you, they may handcuff you but nothing can stop you from thinking: if you are not thinking you do not exist, the thought of a design of a house or a car begins with the thought of the architect, he has to have something on his mind on what he wants it to look like and then work through, the car cannot be created without original thought, I am here to tell someone who is going through a difficult situation that what you have been thinking God is about to create, you have to have an idea how you going to get out of that situation, you got to have something for God to work with and many of the body of Christ are not thinking of anything, they have nothing in their spirits, but God is saying if you have been thinking about something that is bigger than you, something greater than what you are all I need you to do is think about it and get back and let me create it: some of you as you are reading now you are about to create something from your mind that does not match your existence, what you are getting ready is going to shock many people who thought that your life was stuck, who thought that you will never get out of the situation that you are in, what you are thinking will make your enemies wonder and some of you who are not thinking of anything God is about to give you something to think about that is going to drag you out of being normal, and its going to far exceed the expectation of the status quo, and it doesn't even match the structure of your family background, thought ladies and gentleman is the only power on which all things are made, before God spoke anything into existence He had to think, actually God said to Himself let us make a man before He did it He spoke it and before He spoke it He thought it, that's why the enemy loves none thinking believers if he can just get you emotional, shouting, running in church giving people high five but you have no critical thought you are no danger to the enemy's camp, but when you get to the place where you start reevaluating stuff, saying God must have something in store for my life and stop just shouting emotional but shout not for what I have but shout for what you have been thinking. Ladies and gentlemen I want to submit this to you that we live in a thought world, you live in a thought universe, you have a thought existence and you have to make yourself distanced from people who are thoughtless, don't be around people who just want shoes and food but be around people who are thinking outside the box, what you are thinking you are becoming, if you are in any situation and all you think about is how you not going to make it then what you are thinking you are becoming. The bible says the father had two sons and one of them was only thinking about what he could get, you must be careful of people's only angle is about what can benefit them, make no room in your life for people who are only invested in themselves the bible says the younger son went to his father and said give me the share of my inheritance, failing to understand that its not just about me, God did not bless me for me, God blessed me because there are some people depended on me, there are some people whose existence is relying on what I do, because he was thinking it's all about him watch what the bible says Luke 15:14 he spends all he had, people who do not have a passion for other people will go broke buying stuff for themselves, and the text says he spent it all on riotous living, he spend it all why? Because he had no plan, in I remember after getting money from the woman I had sexual relations with all I did was just buy gadgets and spend it all on myself, I had the latest everything with no savings account. He spends all he had after his father gave him everything he asked for, and watch this now he had to go work in a pig pen and this young man was a Jewish boy who came from a rich family and here he is working in a pig pen so he is forced to work with stuff that's beneath him, that does not match the covenant on his life because he has been disobedient to his gift what he got from the father was not what he worked for but because he did not know how to manage his gift he ended up beneath his dignity, some of you are to gifted to be living and working in the environment you in but God in His permissive will He had to allow you to hit rock bottom and you think this is punishment what you are going through right now is not punishment, its not a demonic attack but what you are going through is solitary confinement, God is giving you time out so you may think about how you have been living, how you have ben acting does not line up with how you were raised, you know better than what it is that you have been doing, but somehow you lowered your standard and God said "sit over there for a minute in you are in solitary confinement so you may get yourself together, and in solitary confinement no visitors, you eat but you got no body to eat with, you stuck with yourself, some of you reading this book now you are in solitary confinement there are people around you but you lonely, and in solitary confinement you get tired of praying because you get to the point where you start knowing your own voice, I remember during the time I was experiencing shame many people thought I was being arrogant I just wanted to be alone, I didn't want to talk to many people, I just wanted people to leave me alone because I was in solitary confinement. The prodigal son wakes up in a pig pen and he started to smell like what he works with and the text says "and he thought to himself" sometimes God will shut everything around you cause its obvious you are not thinking and for the first time in his life he starts coming up with a plan, he started thinking what am I going to say to the father, you know when you going through a difficult situation you don't pray the manufactured prayers you have to really think what am I going to say to the father. And not only was he thinking what he was going to say to the father but he was also thinking how did I get to this point? We don't like to take responsibility because we live in a victimization culture look at this the devil didn't spend his money, no con- artist tricked him, he was not a victim of a scheme, but he is the reflection of the absence of discipline. I feel like telling someone that you need a moment to think, it was not your ex's fault it was your fault you were so ignorant because of your loneliness you lowered your standards you knew that that man was not for you, you knew that that woman was not for you, you knew that God had something else for you but you kept forcing yourself on something that didn't line up with his will, he was broke when you met him, you had to pay for the dates, you had to pay for his clothes, you had to pay for his rent, now you angry that the man doesn't pay child support are you really surprised? You knew what kind of man he was

We don't like to take responsibility because we live in a
victimization culture look at this the devil didn't spend his money,
no con- artist tricked him, he was not a victim of a scheme, but
he is the reflection of the absence of discipline

He started thinking how did I get to this point, ladies and gentleman the prodigal son did not just end up in the pit, there were some series of events that happened in my life that got me to where I am, I did not just end up here things happened I took some wrong turns, I passed by the exit when God was trying to show me the way out, I kept going to what God delivered me from, I was like a dog returning to my own vomit but I am Here to tell someone that if you can think of a plan God will deliver you the prodigal son when he was in the pen he was thinking about a plan if I can just get to my father's house I am going to do better than where I am right now, some of you feel like the enemy is after you because of what you have but the enemy is not after you for what you have but the enemy is after what you have been dreaming about and the last thing the enemy wants you to do is get to your father's house because the devil knows if you get to church everything you have been dreaming of will come to pass. so he came up with a plan, I will go to my father's house, he thought of what to say to the father and listen to this, he acknowledged where he was, was his fault and he told himself that when I see the father this is what I am going to say to him, I know I messed up but I am still your child you got to take care of me, I am born of your born, I am flesh of your flesh and your blood runs in my veins, you don't have to put me on the top but you got to do something for me, with a plan in his mind, a dream in his heart, conviction in his spirit, repentance in his prayer he now heads back to the father, heading back to the father the father sees him afar off and the father now starts making his own plans kill the fatted calf, get me a robe, the one that he had lost, get me a ring and while he was coming he had no idea the father has been thinking of him and while the father was thinking about him the father wants more for him than what he expected for himself, I am here to tell you that no matter where you are God has plans for you and the plans that He has for you is not to find you a job, all he wanted was a job but the plans God had for him was to put him in position and the position God was putting him in is as if you didn't sin, I don't see a sinner all I see is my child, I don't see a failure but all I see is a victor, God is thinking about you, you can come back home

It was a road of rejection

Those who will welcome you are more than those who rejected you

Like it or not rejection tries hard to become one of your best friends, because it shows up at the most in opportune time and it always comes without an invitation, rejection has the ability to make you feel anxious, hurt, dejected, and even depressed we all have different tolerance levels for how much rejection we can handle, but what is amazing is that rejection always comes as like an un suspecting vehicle running us over in a hit and run and never pulls over to give its insurance information, everybody at one point of your life you had to deal with the feeling of being rejected unless you put your guard down I am not talking about this week, but you have been going through rejection whether you realize it or not you have been going through rejection your entire life. rejection starts at school when you are not accepted as a part of the popular group, not selected for group activities, ridiculed in the school grounds, and the difficulty of trying to make new friends when the only people you knew was mama and now you thrown in an environment of strangers, you learn the alphabet but nobody taught you the inner person skills, you found out how to count but you didn't know that some people are mean for no reason, its difficult trying to navigate who can I confined in?, who can I trust?, school can become so traumatic that some children will fake sickness just so they don't have to go to school, the intensity of the stress of a school yard experience has the potential of making an extraverted child introverted so the learning disabilities are not necessary because they cannot learn, but because the environment that they in is almost as if they are in maximum prison cell, so their hating of the entire learning educational experience by the time they are 14 years and make such comments like; school is not for me, and if I can ask what did biology ever do to you?, what did mathematics ever did to a learner?, how did geography offend you?, why is reading such a problem?, its not that, it's the people they are forced to learn with and because of that it is impaired there learning process, its amazing to know that some of the most brilliant minds are in jail, it is mind blowing to even phantom that some of the people who have had the highest grades at school are right now walking in the streets of Johannesburg with no place to live, its not because they didn't have the brain, but they were in an environment that rejected them, its one thing to just be rejected at school but what happens ladies and gentleman when you are rejected at home?, abandoned by your parent.

It's strange to know that 57% percent of teenage girls who are impregnated are done so by older age man who are never reported because they were looking for the affection of a father who never visited them and that level of rejection had so much of a pain and affliction on a young man who never saw a man operate in the attributes of God and raised by a mother and a grandmother no wonder the church becomes a magnet for man who are conflicted in their own sexuality because they don't see any man in church worshipping God all they see is a woman putting on stalking's, lip sticks and mascara, and they jump from relationship to relationship looking for love, its critical what rejection can do in a young person's life that's why we need to create an environment in the church for acceptance and allow whosoever, with whatsoever to come and be healed, many people are angry with the world because they got rejected at home, its one thing for me to be rejected at school but its another thing for me to be rejected at home and I know there are those of you who think they had a balanced life at home all was good and school was also good and everything was great until you had to deal with the rejection in a relationship, a partner leaves for someone else without warning you were doing everything you could think to do and then you found out by default you were in a relationship of one because the other person while they were there physically, emotionally they had left a long time ago and you cry looking for that space to be filled, its one thing to be rejected at school, another thing to be rejected at home, something all together different to be rejected in a relationship, what happens when you are rejected on a job?, turned downed on an interview, never got a call back, you loose you promotion over someone who doesn't even have the skills compared to you, fail to operate in your calling seeing others functioning and even though you have something to say but you are sidelined, ladies and gentleman at on point of our lives we all experience different levels of rejection I am here to tell you that your season of rejection is over when they brought Jesus before Pilate this was the costume to set one prisoner free I am here to tell you that this is your season to be free from your rejection, you going to be free from what happened to you at school, free from what happened to you in that house, free from what happened to you in that relationship, what happened to you on that job as a matter of fact the reason they rejected you is because you were better than them now watch this the bible says they brought Jesus and Barabbas on the balcony and because Jesus was all man and God and I am sure as a man he started counting votes and he looks at the crowd and said I know I got this, because five thousand of them I fed with loaves and fish there's no way I am going to be rejected, and I see a woman there in the corner who for years she had an issue of blood and nobody could touch her but I healed her I know she will vote for me, and on the left hand side I see two blind man and I laid hands on them and they recovered, there were people who were in sin and I walked passed them and set them free I know I got this, so they stood the two candidates up Jesus and Barabbas for the vote and Barabbas comes in as the dark horse and everybody starts voting for him this was messing up with Jesus' mind I have been here for three years performing miracles and teaching you and changing your life and when its time for you to step up to the plate you going with somebody new?, the crowd shouted we will take Barabbas and Jesus with one long tear coming down his cheek didn't even protest said take him, that's what you want over me? Take him, see if he will love you the way I loved you?, see if he will do what I used to do, brothers and sisters if Jesus was rejected we all going to experience rejection but thank God that those who will welcome you are more than those that have rejected you, look at how many people who are welcoming Christ in their lives now? They are more than those that rejected him

...Those who will welcome you are more than those who rejected you

Lets look at another story in Judges 11:1-11 the Bible says Jephtah was a mighty man of valor but he was the son of a harlot and his father had another wife and when the sons of that woman grew they chased Jephtah away saying you shall not have no inheritance in our father's house for you are the son of another woman and the bible says Jephtah fled from his brothers and dwelt in the land of Tob and worthless men banded together with him in other words he attracted worthless men with him ladies and gentleman I don't know where you are right now in your life, some of you are in the land of Tob where you have been rejected, either by your family, by the society or by your husband or wife but watch this, Tob means to make better or to make good in other words when he went to Tob God was making him better and what good is it to be in a place of making better and not have anything to make better Jepthah attracted worthless man in other words Jephtah was surrounded by worthless men he is in the land of Tob and all around him there is shame, his reputation is lost, people are talking about him, hhe is an embarrassment in the society, he has been rejected but in all that the valor in him was being put to test now in the land of making better it is in Tob that God works with you making you a better person and they will think that they have rejected you but what they don't know is that God is making you better, He's giving you a new identity, the son of a harlot identity is fading and the valor in him is rising, it is in this place that God gives him a new mindset, it is in this place that God gives and develops your potential to full capacity in order for you to face new challenges because even though Japhtah was a mighty man of valor but he had a crisis of identity whenever he wanted to perform this other thing kept coming up, voices would say you cant be a great preacher look you are the son of a harlot, you cant be a good mother, you cant have a business and all that so he had a crisis of confident he was not so confident and that crippled his gift so what does God do? he causes his brothers to reject him, why would he attract worthless men? Because God was going to use the quality in him to change those man, God became to test his quality of leadership in him the valor is beginning to mature and the son of a harlot vanish and as you are reading some of you are in the land of Tob but I have good news for you because the land of Tob has a time limit watch what the bible says in verse 5 the bible says there was a war in the land and guess what because the land of Tob has a time limit what does the elders do? They went to fetch Jephtah because his time had come, I am here to announce to someone who have been rejected, abandoned that your time has come, the mighty man of valor in you is rising and the son of a harlot is fading now Jephath said I will come with you but you have to make me your leader in other words he was stating his price, I am here to challenge somebody that it doesn't matter that you have failed but you must state your price, I know I have failed but I am a mighty man of God, I know I have failed but I am a might woman of God and so they agreed with him and Jephath became their leader and the whole city welcomed him those who will welcome you are more than those who have rejected you, there is a way out, hold on Tob has a time limit.

It was a road of confusion

"And when he came to himself, he said, how many
hired servants of my father's have bread enough and to
spare, and I perish with hunger! – Luke 15:17

Jephath is confused because he finds himself in a place that he can't understand why his own family, his own brothers would be the ones to reject him? if I can be rejected by outsiders then I don't have a problem but rejected by my own family, the ones that I am suppose to feel safe when I am around them are the ones that are rejecting me in the book of acts 12:12-15 the church had been praying for Peter so that he can be released and after God miraculously set him free from prison Peter went to the house of Mary, the mother of John whose surname was Mark, where many were gathered together praying, here is a church praying for Peter that he may be released into his full potential and when God starts doing that the church the very same people who were praying for him are the very ones that when Peter came and started knocking on the door, the doors of opportunity, doors of breakthrough, doors of business deals, doors of pressing for a better life doubts him watch this, Peter is knocking at the gate and a girl named Rhoda came to answer the door and when she recognized Peter's voice she didn't even open the door, but ran in and announced that Peter stood before the gate, be careful of the Rhoda's in the church when you begin to pursue God, knocking at every door you find they will be waiting at the door so that every move you make they will tell the church, they are the ones that gossip about every move that you make, but watch this Peter is knocking at the door, he is pressing on for a blessing, he's attending every church service, he's doing all he can to get inside because he is coming from prison and he is tired of being in prison the church's prayers are working now finally he has been released then as he knocks Rhoda runs and tells the church and what does the church do? They say to Rhoda you are crazy, you have lost your mind it's not Peter it's a angel in other words its not real, because the Peter that we know is in prison, the Peter that we know is bound, the Peter that we know does not have this potential to be free cause he is locked up, the Peter that we know comes from a poor background and its not possible for him to have that Job, its not possible for him to be on television, its not possible for him to own that the Peter we know is bound, you are out of your mind how is that possible? Now watch this Peter is knocking at the door and Rhoda hears that it's Peter but here is Rhoda's problem she runs and tells the church, and the church says she is out of her mind, she is crazy in other words Rhoda's problem is she is connected to people that can pray for something but they don't have the faith to possess it because the church that's been praying for Peter and Peter is knocking at the door and the church wont get up to open it, it's a picture of a people that can pray for something but they cant possess it, they can pray but they cannot possess, because when Rhoda said Peter is at the door they said you are crazy, you have lost your mind, then they said its just an angel they don't want you to believe its real, but I am here to tell you that its real what God is about to do in your life its real, all this confusion that I have they are about to end, I might not understand, I might be confused but one thing I know is that if I can just keep knocking the door God is about to end my confusion, now here is the saddest thing when the people that's suppose to protect you the people that's suppose to make you feel welcome don't open the door for you, they said its an angel, in other words its not real but thank God that Peter kept knocking and when they opened and saw it was real it was Peter they were astonished, those that prayed for you but never believe you can make it are about to be astonished God is about o use their prayers to astonish them

It was a road of decision

"I will arise and go to my father, and say unto him, father, I
have sinned against heaven, and before thee! – Luke 15:18

He had to make a decision after all to go home and that decision he made was not the same as the decision he made before he left home, now he was in a position to make the right decision its so important to make the right decisions in life not just make decisions the bible says in Joel 3:14 "Multitudes, multitudes in the valley of decision: for the day of the Lord is near in the valley of decision" many people are in the valley of decision because in life we one way or the other have to make a decision, we going to have to make a decision of who to marry, we going to make a decision on what to do when you find ourselves in trouble am going to just sit here and cry? or should I rise and go to my father? Before I was suspended at church if I would have made a right decision of not sleeping with the woman I wouldn't have been suspended so I made a decision of sleeping with her and not make a decision of not sleeping even though I made a decision but it was a wrong decision so I encourage you before you can do anything in your life make a decision to make the right decisions at all times even though you are in the valley but you can still make a right decision because the day of the Lord is near in the valley of decision

It was road of fear

Fearing of the unknown what will my father say or do when I go home was he going to accept me, this is the fear that has crippled the body of Christ the fear of being judged, the fear of being rejected by God because of your sin, the fear of the unknown will I make it in life?, what is in store for my life? The prodigal son had a fear in him after spending all he had and he's living in a foreign land how was I going to make it in a place that I don't know

It was a road that seemed not to end

"And not many days after the younger son gathered all together, and took his journey into a far country, and there wasted his substance with riotous living" – Luke 15:13

Have you ever been in a situation that doesn't seem to end? The bible says he was in a far country far from home, far from his family even if he had missed them he couldn't be with them cause he was in a far country, far from everything that he was used to, have you ever been in a far country? Where you don't feel the love of God anymore, you can't pray like you used to even though you pray but you feel you're in a far country? For twelve years the bible says the woman with the issue of blood was in the road that never seemed to end twelve years she tried everything and not only did it seem not to end but she grew worse and worse in that situation but every situation has a time limit, weeping may endure for a night but joy comes in the morning, just hold on even if it feels like its not ending help is on the way

It was a road of love

"And he arose, and came to his father. But when he was yet
a great way off, his father saw him, and had compassion, and
ran, and fell on his neck, and kissed him! – Luke 15:20

And he arose, and came to his father. But when he was yet a great way off, his father saw him, and had compassion, and ran, and fell on his neck, and kissed him. I want you to know that no matter what situation you are in, no matter what you have done, or what you did not do, God's love is available for you, and you can get up and go to the father. What do you give to someone that you love? Gifts, money? Or presents? And what will God give you to show His love for you? He will give Himself because if He gives you anything other than Himself then He seizes to love the prodigal son even though he had messed up and was lost but his father's love was always there for him, the love was there from the beginning while he was still in the father's house before he left and the love was there even when he left, so the father's love was there in the beginning and it was there in the end, notice what it says "But when he was a great way off, his father saw him and had compassion and ran, and fell on his neck, and kissed him" this portion of scripture is mind blowing now let me tell you something that will mess you up in the Jewish culture for a man to reveal his knees was considered to be disgraceful especially a man of his caliber a rich Jewish farmer that's why they had to cover their knees with the long robes that they wore, now in order for the father to run to his son means he had to pull up the robe because you cant run in that robe, so he had to pull it up that means he didn't care about being disgraced for the sake of his son, he didn't care of loosing his dignity because of his son, he didn't care loosing his reputation because of the son the bible says he ran to his son

In other words he was saying I would rather be disgraced so that you may find grace, I would rather loose my reputation so you may get yours back ladies and gentleman I don't know about you but this makes me jump and excited knowing that there is nothing that I can do that the father cant reach out to me. I have heard people praying in difficult times "Lord I need more of your love" because while they going through what they going through they feel like God is not with them but I am here to tell you that the bible says in Romans 5:5 "the Love of God is shed abroad in our hearts by the Holy Spirit which is given to us" in other words God's love is always there and all you need is to tap into the love that is always there, when the prodigal son went away his father never stopped loving him even though he was away but when he came home he was in a position to receive and experience the love his father always had for him, if I tell you that I love you and you don't believe me you will never receive and experience the love that I have for you, God's love is always there for us we need to tap into it, believe it and receive it then we will experience it, when the prodigal son came home he was able to receive and experience the love his father always had for him, his father never stopped loving him and that is what made him to go home that love, he said my father is a good man I will arise and go back home, it was his father's love that compelled him to go home. Pastor John Hagee shared a true powerful story of a six year old boy standing in the front of the pet store, his nose is pressed against the window and he's looking at the pets his eyes starring to a black and white spotted puppy that's jumping around in the display window and the little boy goes into the store and he puts his 75 cents down the counter and he tells the owner of the store "I will buy that dog" and the owner of the store says "son that dog cost over 300 dollars and his little shoulders sink with absolutely disappointment then the mother dog came trotting out of the pet groom with four black white puppies right behind her but there was another puppy about four or five paces behind her limping and dragging its back legs to keep up the little boy pointed to the lame puppy and said "I want that one and the pet store owner said "son you don't want that dog because it was born without a hip socket that dog will never be able to run, jump or do the fun things you like to do so you surely wouldn't want that dog and the little boy reached down and pulled up his trousers he pointed to the heavy steel braces on both sides of his legs that ran up to his knees he had polio the little boy pointed to his legs and said with tears in his eyes I need that puppy because that puppy understands me and I can understand that puppy" that's how God looks at us with the eyes of love He saw us crippled in sin broken, hopeless, in shame, bound and said I want that one whose life is broken that one who has been crippled by circumstances, that one who has been rejected, that one who's dreams has been crushed, that one who's going through a divorce and thinks there is no future for them, that one who feels like a failure, that one who's hurt has been broken by the death of the spouse, that one that's in sin and sickness cause I can forgive sin and I can heal every disease, I will take that one that's living in disgrace, that one that thinks there life is over. God is looking at your potential not your past, don't let your past determine your future some of you are looking at the time you failed all of us has failed, if you have failed get over it everybody has, if you're a prodigal son or a prodigal daughter get up from the mud go back to your father's house your past ended last night your future begins today God is love and God loves you. Whatever mistakes you made, whatever crime you in lift up your head and rejoice the best is yet to come because there is a God in heaven who has all power in heaven and earth He can move mountains for you, He will make the crooked ways straight, He will defeat your enemies before you

It was a road of contradiction

And he went and joined himself to a citizen of that country;
and he sent him into his fields to feed swine 16: and he
would fain have filled his belly with the husks that the swine
did eat: and no man gave unto him _Luke 15:15-16

I discovered that its in the times of contradiction that God shows Himself more in our lives, here is a contradiction this young man is a son of a Jewish rich farmer even though he had failed his father his son ship never changed and here he is living below his reputation, living below who he was feeding swine and even eating what the swine eats and yet at his father's house there was plenty of food and even his father's servants didn't eat that kind of food so here is a young Jewish boy walking in contradiction, but when he came to himself he went back to his father and after all that he had done he gets home and here is another contradiction after he got home the father loved him, gave him the best despite of what he had done, isn't God suppose to bless me when I have done good? That was a contradiction to be blessed after he had messed up that's why the other son was angry he couldn't understand why his father could do that? even him he also walked the road of contradiction after he had been a loyal son, never demanded anything from his father stayed home and did all the work expecting a blessing but he didn't get anything. Now here is a powerful thing about contradiction the prodigal son got the ring the bull after he walked in contradiction and the other son even though he had been given also his share but he never discovered it until he walked in contradiction he was a good boy at home did all he was asked but he never realized what he had until he also walked in contradiction so it was the prodigal son's return that made him discover what he had, in the mess that you are in sometimes you don't see what you have until you rise up and go home then you will discover what you already have and many will also discover what they have through your rising up and limping your way home so I want to encourage you that you might be down but rise up and limp your way home the father is waiting for you to shower you with his love and gifts, its amazing that the bible says the son after asking his father for his inheritance the father gave him but he also kept another portion knowing that the son will spend all and come back so in other words whatever you have spent, some of you might be saying I have spend my reputation, I have spend my dignity, I have spend my gift but I am here to say to you God never runs out of anything He has kept whatever you lost and it's fat

It was a road of repentance

"I will arise and go to my father, and will say unto him, Father, I have sinned against heaven and before thee" – Luke 15:18

Whatever you went through or you going through if you don't repent then you will never make it home the father is waiting for you at home the father never stopped loving him but he had to repent and show remorse on what he had done so that the father can accept him home, the bible says in 1 John 1:9 "if we confess our sins, he is faithful and just to forgive us our sins, and to cleanse us from all unrighteousness" there is no sin that God cannot forgive and there is no sin that the blood of Jesus cannot wash whatever you going through now you can still go back home the father is waiting for you with wide open arms

It was a road of brokenness

"And the younger of them said to his father, Father
give me the portion of goods that falleth to me. And
he divided unto them his living– Luke 15:12

Now I want you to see how God works at times in our lives the bible tells us that after the son went home the father made a great party for him, the father gave him a ring and a seal of approval to me that's promotion, that's elevation because he never had those things before he left home so I believe before God can entrust you with elevation He has to break you first and its in the brokenness that you are multiplied you remember the story of the little with two fish and 5 loaves of bread what's ironic to me in this in this story is that they had counted the woman and the children and yet the one who was not counted was the one who had the miracle isn't it amazing that God uses people that other people don't count they were so busy counting who they thought was significant that they didn't count the very one that God had moved into the position to release a blessing that was needed, God will always use something that was not counted to produce the miracle. Then the little boy brings his lunch that the mother had packed for him two fish and five loaves of bread and Jesus takes the two fish and five loaves of bread commands the disciples to have the crowds sit down into groups of fifty this had to take sometime for hungry people five thousand men not to mention the children and woman and they were hungry and I am sure some of them were about to faint and Now they have to wait for the order of sitting arrangements to take place I want to just say this "the best miracles in your life take time, they cannot be driven by hunger or need, or necessity sometimes you have to get yourself structured and in order so that you are ready to receive the magnitude of what God has for you, just because you have a driving need doesn't mean you have to disperse the time, the order and the structure that God wants you to have before He elevates you wait on what God wants to do. some people are so busy trying to get what God has that they don't provide the structure that is necessary to sustain what they have been given. The bible says the younger son came to his father and said "father, give me the portion of goods that falleth to me" in other words this young man couldn't wait he was in a hurry to get elevated without building a structure that will help him sustain what he was about to get, that's the problem with the church we are gifts minded we run with the gifts and forget character one man of God said "your gift will take you there but your character will keep you there" here is a young man all he wanted was his inheritance and if you read the historical commentaries concerning this incident the scholars said "for a younger son to ask his father for his inheritance while the father was still alive in the Jewish culture it was an insult it was as though he was wishing his father to die. And what does the father do? Even though he knew that it was not yet time for the younger son to get his portion because he was not structured, he was not matured enough to handle that kind of wealth the father knew about that but what does he do in order to solve the problem? He gave him his inheritance but that was not all that he wanted to give him that was not all that he had in mind so he kept the best that he wanted to offer him and allowed him to go in other words he was about to take him on a journey of brokenness where he was going to break him and teach him so that he can mature and be structured to handle the elevation that was soon to come upon his life. Now in our story of the two fish and five loaves of bread the bible says after they were all seated in other words after there was a structure then the miracle took place the miracle didn't take place while they were not seated and structured but when they were all seated Jesus took the bread and fish and blessed it and this is amazing Jesus is blessing something that is not enough! And he took it and he blessed it notice we knew how many loaves Jesus had we knew how much fish Jesus had but when he broke it that's when we lost count. The blessing is in the breaking that which refuses to be broken refuses to be blessed it is the breaking of life that produces the blessing of life; I know a lot of you will not understand this because you yourself have not been broken but I have noticed in my life that the most blessed people I have ever met in my life have gone through something that broke them, the blessing is in the breaking and the more he broke it, the more it multiplied and we cannot keep count of it because every time he broke it, it multiplied in his hands, every time you went through all the stuff that you went through God was not punishing you, He was blessing you, every time you felt abandoned, every time they talked bad about you, every time they betrayed you, every time they persecuted me they thought they were cursing me but they were wrong, God was blessing me, and the father knowing that in order for his son to get the seal of approval, in order for him to get the ring and the fatted calf he had to allow him to go through brokenness the bible says not after long the son gathered all the father had given him and he went to a far country and spend all that he had with riotous living in other words because he was not matured and structured he couldn't manage what his father gave him so he spent all and there arose a famine in that land that he began to be in want but no one would give him anything, have you ever be in a place of want? A place where no body gives you anything? That's the place of brokenness where God starts breaking you so that you may not trust in people or trust in your job but trust in Him so God began to deal with him and the bible says 'he came to his senses and that's exactly what the father wanted for him to come to his senses that's the place of maturity, that's the structured place where you suddenly realize that what you did was wrong, what you did was not worth it and that there is still hope for you that's where God wants us to be but we have to go through brokenness in order for some of us to realize that, how would I have known that God can forgive if I never sinned?, how would I have realized that God can multiple me if I never lacked? Whatever you going through it's a blessing because it is in there where God multiplies you

It was a road of lack

"And he would fain have filled his belly with the husks that the swine did eat: and no man gave unto him – Luke 15:16

When you are in this road you lack because the psalmist said the Lord is my shepherd and I shall not want that means when you make God your shepherd then you won't lack but notice the prodigal son had left his father that's why he lacked because without the father's presence you cannot make it he was in a place where the father was not that's why he started to lack because the bible says there arose a famine and he became to be in want"

It was a road of guilt

There's a difference between guilt and shame; the terms "guilt and "shame" can be understood in two ways. Objectively, guilt refers to our culpability as people who have broken God's law, which results in punishment, death, and God's Judgment. Subjectively, guilt is experienced as the burden of responsibility for transgressing a moral boundary. We feel it as pangs of conscience, as blame or self-accusation when we know the offense is our fault. Guilt is the inexcusability we feel for our sins. Objectively, shame is like pollution in our relationship with God; the uncleanness of our sin clashes with God's holiness. It is the dishonor and marring of the image of God caused by sin. Subjectively, shame is our sense of defilement in the presence of the holy God. It is our painful realization that as sinners we are naked before God Genesis 3:7. Unwanted visibility and the desire to conceal are at the of the shame response. Guilt is our sense that we have gone too far, but shame is feeling that we have not gone far enough. It is a sense of moral failure that leads to embarrassment, feelings of unworthiness, and despair. Guilt feelings focus on what we do, whereas shame feelings focus on who we are, how we look, and how we relate to others. The answers to objectively guilt are punishment and restitution a balancing of accounts. The answer to objective shame is covering what is exposed, exchanging the shame for honor or glory, and restoring relationships. The answer to both subjective guilt and subjective shame is love, love that forgives, and love that affirms, honors, and restores broken relationships

Guilt and shame in the Bible

The threads of shame and guilt both appear already in the story of Adam and Eve's first sin in Genesis 3. Their first reaction was one of shame. "the eyes of both of them wee opened, and they realized they were naked; so they sewed fig leaves together and made coverings for themselves," in answer to God's question, "where are you?" Adam said, "I was afraid because I was naked; so I hid," before they sinned, Adam and Eve "were both naked and they felt no shame," after they sinned they covered themselves, we were afraid, and hid – three typical characteristics of the shame reaction. God's response introduces the thread of guilt: "who told you that you were naked? Have you eaten from the tree that I commanded you not to eat from? After establishing their guilt, God punished them. But in the promise of victory over the serpent through the seed of the woman and the provision of better garments for their bodies, God hinted at the marvelous answer to guilt and shame that would come in Jesus Christ. Later in the old Testament God called for purification ceremonies and guilt offerings that also pointed toward the final solution to our guilt and shame dilemma. Jesus's death on the cross was a perfect answer to our guilt problem. "God made him who had no sin to be sin for us, so that in him we might become the righteousness of God 2 Corinthians 5:21. Jesus's crucifixion was also a perfect answer to our shame problem. He "endured the cross despising its shame Hebrews 12:2 on the cross our naked savior took responsibility for our spiritual nakedness. And now, with the veil of the temple torn, we can approach our holy God without shame. To all who believe in Him he offers white clothes to cover our shameful nakedness Revelation 3:18. He not only covers our shame; he exchanges our shame for a glory that reflects his own. Jesus referred to his death as the hour of his glorification John 12:23, in taking responsibility for our sin on the cross, he transformed the cross from a symbol of shame into a symbol of glory. Guilt and shame are not only aspects of God's punishment of our sin. They are also grace filled provisions designed to move us to godly sorrow, which brings repentance that leads to salvation 2 Corinthians 7:10. They function together in a healthy way to motivate people of all cultures to seek God's gracious forgiveness and reconciliation

It was a road of condemnation

A lot of believers hear condemning thoughts, and some people even think its God telling them these things, my friend, nothing could be further from the truth! God never tells you what a loser you are, Jesus said He came not to condemn the world but to save it John 12:47. Condemnation comes from Satan and is meant to tear you down, condemnation continually points out what a failure you are, and how badly you've messed up, and condemnation is showing you the problem but avoiding the solution

It was a road of trouble

"And when he had spent all, there arose a mighty famine in that land; and he began to be in want" Luke 15:4

There is a story that a certain man of God shared of a certain famous lady who was an exchange student in Italy her room mate was discovered murdered and she immediately became the prime suspect she served four years of a twenty five year sentence before she was released but while she was incasorated for four years if you can imagine four years in solitary confinement but to add insult to injury she is locked up with people that don't speak her language, I remember the time that I was in trouble after being suspended of all my pastoral duties and here I was I had lost my voice, my influence and there was nothing that I would say that people would listen, this woman even though she tried to speak but the people she was locked up with didn't understand her language now here is a question how was she going to communicate? So she had to go through the emotional trauma of having no connection to anybody that she was with and further more they were not speaking the same language, it was said that in her first week of incasaration the prison warden lied about her that she was HiV positive after they did some tests and they requsted her to write down a list of people that she had slept with and the warden of the prison sold that story to the newspaper and had all her lovers listed knowing that she was not HIV positive so for four years she is living in a cell thinking she is dying not knowing that she still has some years left, she didn't have any friends, her family couldn't afford to come visit her, and every night one of the jail guards comes in her cell trying to ask her for sexual favors so in her mind she thinks she has to spend twenty five years in her heart she thinks she has HIV and in her spirit she thinks she has been forgotten and without any warning she was called back in the court and they said everything that they had against her was circumstantial and as a consequence we going to release you so she was released and she flew back to her country and she was trying to go on with her life hoping to start a family of her own and finish her degree and after a month enjoying her freedom the high court said we changed our mind sent her back here this was her response mumbling to herself "I cant take another trial" this is what really moved me in her story the statement that she made "I cant take another trial" some of you as you are reading you have been through a lot in your life and you just cant go through it again, if only you knew what it is that I had to go through and how many times the enemy pressed me into a corner, can you imagine what I had to go through especially the moments they called the pastors to come forward and pray for people in the church and I know well that I am a pastor but couldn't go forward, can you imagine sitting down the whole service and not say anything and yet you had something to say brothers and sisters it was hard for me and I say like that woman "I cant take another trial" I wouldn't want to go through the same thing again. If I can be honest with you it was not a good situation to be but I thank God that His hand is upon my life, if I can be honest with you "I cant take another trial" whatever you do if I got to stand trial don't make me go back there, I don't want to be in that place I know how it feels, I know how it feels to be suspended of all your duties, to be in an environment where nobody wants me to win, in a place where nobody speaks my language in an atmosphere of rejection, but thank God for His grace and mercy the prodigal son found himself in trouble all his money was gone, there was a famine in the land and he found himself alone, no friends, no family, no job and he joined himself to a farmer who sent him to work with swine and he gave him no food to a point where he started eating the food of the swine he was in trouble because of the decision he made

It was a dark road

"the first day of the week cometh Mary Magdalene
early, when it was dark, unto the sepulcher, seeth the
stone taken away from the sepulcher" John 20:1

The text says while it was dark she went to the tomb, there are couple of things that I need to alert you that this Mary in the text is not the mother of Jesus but this Mary is the one of ill repute, she had a bad reputation she had a stained character because she had spent most of her life sleeping with people and not loving people, she was living a life in the dark the bible says she went to the tomb while it was dark, because she was used to living in the dark, she had a reputation of being a harlot, a loose woman, of low standards because she needed company to be complete because their was a void in her heart she always needed somebody in bed with her in order to make sure she fills that void but something happened when she had an encounter with God, when she had an encounter with God her passion changed, her desires changed, her habits changed how do we know that? because every other time when she was in the dark she had somebody with her but now in John 20 when she was in the dark she didn't take any body she goes by herself, she goes while its still dark all by herself, the text says other woman went to the tomb looking for the risen savor but the difference between them and Mary the other woman showed up when the sun came up but she came running while it was still dark and she saw the stone had been moved she took of running, watch this! She never looked into the tomb all she saw was the stone was moved and she ran why did she run? She ran because she didn't want to be anyway where God's presence was not, I want to help someone here you have to run if you find yourself in a place where God's presence is not but the problem we have in the church we love the dark places imagine the prodigal son he is living in a light the rest of his life but in the back of his mind he is thinking about how he can go to the dark because he has been told that its nice in the dark, where you sleep with woman in the church without anyone finding out, I am here to tell you to run, and when she ran look what happened she ran to Peter and Peter took of running as well when Mary gave Peter her testimony Peter ran I want to tell somebody that when you run away from temptation and you tell others then they will also run away. Many people are living in the dark even though they come to church and look like Christians but they living in the dark the prodigal son when it was darker in his life he decided to go back home you can still go home no matter how dark it is in your life there is a light that came

into the world that you may have light that's Christ Jesus he can deliver
you from all trouble

It was a road of restoration

"But the father said to his servants, bring forth the best robe, and put
it on him; and put a ring on his hand, and shoes on his feet, and bring
the fatted calf, and kill it; and let us eat, and be merry" Luke 15:22-23

In Acts 12 from verse 5 we see a very interesting story that I want to
share with you in this chapter that no matter what you have lost God will
restore you. I want you to notice verse number 5 of the book of Acts 12 the
bible says that Peter was kept in prison but I want you quickly pay attention
to this phrase "that prayer was made" many people think prayer is simply
prayed but we have to understand that prayers have to be made but not just
simply prayed but they have to be made its very interesting that when you
study the shadows and types in the old testament you look at the way they
made the incense the incense its very interesting that even in the book of
Psalms the bible says that the morning and the evening prayers are sent up
to God like incense and the bible says when he made the incense he had the
calumus, cassias and the cinnamon and he says everything that he put in it
had to be of equal weight, Revelation 5:8 says that it came up before God
as a sweet smelling odor and God holds them in a vowel and Revelation 8:4
says that once He gets enough of the sweet smelling odor in His vowel then
He throws it back to earth, but He has to smell it and He actually smells
for the ingredients that has been put in and what ingredients is He smelling
for? Philippians 4:6 says when we pray it should be prayer, it should be
supplication, it should be making your request known unto God watch this!
With thanksgiving, just like there was callamus, and cassias and cinnamon
a little pinch of this and a little pinch of this you had to have equal weight
when you pray God smells He is sniffing for to make sure you have prayer,
you have supplication, your request be made known but He also smells for
with thanksgiving and God says when you make your prayer, when you mix
your prayers I don't want a lot of request to much request and not enough
thanksgiving this thing has to be balanced, it has to have equal weight of

ingredients so in other words my point is to let you know that prayers have to be made not prayed and here is Peter in prison he is in prison and James has just been beheaded now don't get to sad over that because I found out in order for you to go on in God, to go all the way deeper in Him it will cause you to loose your head, for the bible says in the book of James a double minded person which means two minds, two heads is unstable in all his ways and that person should not think that he is going to receive anything from God, you cannot have your mind competing against the mind of Christ one head has to go and the head of the church which is Christ is not going anywhere and so you got to be willing to loose your head let me take you to the deep end of the pool its very interesting that the bible says Elizabeth is carrying John the Baptist in her womb and she is six months ahead of Mary and Mary just got pregnant and she has Jesus in her womb now watch this! John the Baptist is in an unconscious state when John the Baptist encounters Jesus, Jesus has just been conceived in the womb of Mary but when Elizabeth walks up to Mary belly to belly, womb to womb the bible says that John the Baptist leaps in the womb of Elizabeth why is there a leap? because now he understands his purpose what good is a forerunner without Jesus? He doesn't understand why he has to get six months ahead and he doesn't understand why he has to prepare a way for Jesus but if there is no Jesus there is no need for a forerunner he is not the train he is just simply the train conductor who stands outside the train and tells everybody else to get on and he is not the way, he is the voice of one calling in the wilderness repent for the kingdom of God is at hand and so if there is no Jesus then John the Baptist's purpose makes no sense so when he meets Jesus in the womb of Mary he gets excited because now he has a purpose, now he understands what he is, why he is, who he is and so he leaps but he is in an unconscious state watch this! The same John the Baptist now in a jail cell in a conscious state sends his disciples to Jesus and says I want you to go ask Him is He really the one or should we be looking for another? How could you be in an unconscious state in Elizabeth's womb as an infant and you have no problem you leap, you recognize that it is Jesus and you leap, you get excited but now you are a grown man you have preached and said "get ready for the kingdom of God is at hand" but in a jail cell going through trials and tribulations and you are about to be beheaded yourself and all of a sudden now you have to seek word and sent word out that I need to find out whether he is the one or should we be looking for another can I tell you what the problem is? Now the problem is logical and reason has got in the way, brethren if you not careful your mind will stand in between you and your Jesus, your logic will get in the way of your faith there is somebody reading this book and you believing God for something and the only thing that's blocking you is that your logic and your reason you trying to instead of believing God you trying to figure God out, you want to know how God is going to do it? And all God is trying to tell you is that He is going to do it, God doesn't speak to you in explanation He speaks to you in declarations, oh my God I feel like preaching and tell somebody that God is about to restore you some of you want God to come and explain to you how He is going to pay your bills, how He is going to get you out of that circumstance, God will not explain to you but He will declare it to you, so if you trying to figure God out you will miss God sometimes God will tell you to move and it will make no sense to you, sometimes God will tell you to go and apologize to people who you think owes you an apology, sometimes God doesn't make sense. So you have to be willing to loose your mind to get the mind of Christ because a double minded person is unstable in their ways and they wont receive anything from God and the Bible says verse 6 that Peter is sleeping between four soldiers after Herod had brought him to prison and the thing is this you can always tell what's on your life by what's trying to hold you, sometimes you can tell what's in your life by what the enemy sends after you, some of you the reason people at your work had to lie about you, had to talk bad about you, had to reject you is because they are persecuting you for where you going and not where you are and sometimes you have to talk back to the enemy, look him in the eyes and say "listen I appreciate the job and everything but let me help you if you want me out of here you don't understand the whole place might shut down, you don't understand what's on my life, I might be the only person in here keeping the doors open because He promised me and I have never seen the righteous forsaken and their children begging for bread, the Lord is my shepherd and I shall not want so walk me out here all you want to, I didn't get hired I was planted here the kingdom of heaven is a like a man who takes seeds and he plants them in his field and the bible says the seeds are the children of the kingdom I didn't get hired I was planted in this field and he shall be like a tree planted by the rivers of water and he shall bring forth his fruit in it's season, you mess with me the whole river will dry up! Now Peter is sleeping between soldiers but look at his condition he is bound with chains Peter is sleeping now the church has preached to people that whatever you going through you have to sleep, and forget the situation you are in God will take care of you, when people abuse you go to sleep, but that's not the truth the only thing I get out of this is to be comfortable in dysfunction that's what's wrong with the church now people are in bondage and they comfortable, people are in chains but they comfortable in their chains, they come to church every week but comfortable, how can you sleep and yet you in bondage, yoked, in an abusive situation but go home and sleep in it, somebody threatens to destroy your life and you sleep in it, you remember Samson? She said to him "tell me what makes you so strong?" one translation actually says "tell me where I can afflict you" the first time you ask me that how can you hurt me? That's the indication I need to get away from you but you can become comfortable in a dysfunctional situation, some of you as you are reading you are verbally abused they call you all kinds of names and you comfortable in dysfunctional situation imagine Peter the chains when they were put on him first time they hurt him and now he got used to them, drugs and alcohol, bitterness, unforgiving spirit and you comfortable in it, you see the church doesn't want to take about all this people struggling with sexual sins, sexual purity and you sleeping don't know when the Lord may come back but I am sleeping. We are comfortable in dysfunction and the problem is we don't know when all this stuff that we have been carrying and hiding on the inside may erupt like a volcano, what do you do when you are in chains? Now the Bible says that an angel had to come in there and shine a light and the light speaks of revelation sometimes God has to take the light from heaven and shines it on our souls and if there is anything on me that's not of you take it out no body is perfect but you have to want to be. Now the angel shines the light and obviously Peter sees his shadow and the reason why God sometimes makes you see your shadow is because He is reminding you that you not God, because 1 John 1 says in Him there is no darkness at all so when God allows you to see your shadow that means everywhere you go you have darkness all around you to remind you that you not God so stop trying to handle all your problems but the way you get a shadow is a light has to hit an object so anytime you find yourself dealing with a shadow or dealing with darkness all you have to do is climb the shadow if you climb the shadow long enough you will run into the object so if you dealing with darkness in your life don't get stuck in the darkness keep climbing till you get the object and Jesus is the light of the world he will restore you hold on where you are light is about to shine, now Peter arises and the angel said put on your sandals on and throw your garment on which means he is not out of the prison yet but he must act like he is out before he came out, now most of us we are in a situation right now but I am here to tell somebody not to sleep in that situation but to act like you are not in that situation, you got to like you have a job before you get a job, you have to look like you have money before you get money put your scandals and get ready to go somewhere, I might not know where I am going but I am getting ready to go somewhere and you know why because the steps of a good man are ordered by the Lord and he did not say the journey of a good man but the steps of a good man because the problem we have in the church people are trying to know the journey but God leads us step by step if you take one step God will give you another step some of you are waiting for a miracle and the angels said throw your garment in other words the garment of praise sometimes you have to praise your way out while you are in that situation praise God in that situation and God will turn it around for you. You have to praise God for healing before you get it, you have to praise God for a breakthrough before you get it, you got to start thanking God for favor before favor manifest on your life. But the thing is before you shout you have to get through these two first gates verse 10 says you got to get through the first gate and the second gate but the third one will open by itself in other words God is saying if you pass the two gates then then the third one is on me, I will open the gate that will lead to the whole city so Peter passed the first and the second and he got to the iron gate that leads to the city and it opened on its own why will it open on its own? So that no man will take credit for this one the third one God is saying I am going to get the glory for number three why number three? Because God thinks in threes, He unveils His will in threes, He unveils His purpose and agenda in threes and the thing about God's threes is that the third dimension is always the greatest so God ordained that time will be set up in threes, past present but the greatest is the future, Corinthians says "Now there abideth faith, hope and love but the greatest of these is love, Jesus says I am the way, the truth and the life but the greatest is on the emphasis of life because he says I came that you might have life and have it more abundantly, you remember the book of Ruth? The whole book of Ruth revolves around three woman, three types of mindsets, theirs is Opah that goes back, there is Naomi that only goes half was cause she is bitter, but there's Ruth the third that presses all the way, God thinks in threes Joseph had three striping's the first striping was when his brothers took the coat of, off him, the second one was when he ran out of Potiphar's house and his wife was holding the next one, but the third striping was the greatest that's when he had to shave and take of the prison clothes himself because he was getting ready to go from the prison to the palace, I am here to tell you that God thinks in threes, He unveils His plan and purpose in threes and they went after having passed the first two gates and there is something that I want to reveal to you about the first two gates in verse 11 of Acts 12 it says "when Peter had to come to himself, he said, Now I know of a surety, that the Lord has sent his angel, and has delivered me out of the hand of Herod, and from all the expectation of the people of the Jews" the first gate you have to get through is Herod's gate that's the attack of the enemy, the second gate that you have to get through is the expectation of people if you can make it through these two gates the third one will open by itself and you going to be open up to unlimited blessings. This young man said I will arise and go back to my father and I don't care what people will say because the last time I looked you didn't wake me up this morning, you didn't hang on no cross, you didn't bleed for me, you didn't die for me, you didn't rise up for me, I will rather please God than please man as long as God is pleased with me I am okay. God is getting ready to open the third gate for me I am about to walk in places that I have never walked before restoration is coming my way, I am about to walk in new dimensions not seasons because seasons are temporally but new dimensions.

CHAPTER FIVE

Covered in shame

"And a certain woman, which had an issue of blood twelve years; and had suffered many things of many physicians, and had spent all that she had, and was nothing bettered but rather grew worse" Mark 5:25-34

This woman with an incurable ceaseless blood flow was in doubt covered in shame. Firstly, it was shameful enough to be a woman in that place at that time for it was a male dominated society; women were expected to remain at home in seclusion. The law deemed women inferior in all matters and expected them to be submissive. In a prayer which Jewish men prayed each day, they thanked God that they had not been born women. Secondly, women on menses or with bleeding disorders were ostracized from society because in the Levitical law, they were considered ritually unclean and untouchable this woman had suffered from bleeding for twelve years therefore she was regarded as ritually unclean and untouchable, her condition was shameful since she was still under the dispensation of the law. It was shameful in keeping with the stringent Levitical laws on ceremonial cleansing and cleanliness. She couldn't sacrifice at the temple because she'd contaminate it, she couldn't even touch anyone or be touched by anyone because that would contaminate them this woman bless her heart she was covered in shame and imagine she had to live for twelve years in that condition the bible says she was loosing blood all the time she kept loosing, she went to doctors but still loosing, have you ever joined a support group but still loosing, you have a good prayer life but still loosing, you attend all church services but still loosing, she's been ostracized by friends who didn't mind being with her if she was healed, but now they have created a hedge of distant because nobody wants to be around a looser and somehow or another she hears that Jesus is coming to town and something starts moving on her inside, and according to Leviticus she cant even leave in her own house, her husband cannot even touch her, (do you have an idea how it feels to have a husband and stay with your husband and he doesn't even touch you?, to have kids and they don't even touch you,) for twelve years she had to go through this, imagine the husband saying this is not even in our family where did you get this? Church people won't even talk to her, for twelve years she is in fear; am I going to die like this? But I want you to notice with me a scripture that messed me up in this story Luke 8:44 says **she came from behind** and touched Jesus. God wants me to tell you that: she came from behind: to tell those who have been fighting, through depression, shame, through suffering and loosing that if you begin to worship me it's the beginning of a season in your life where you **come from behind** I am getting ready to turn the tables over, the anointing upon your life is a come from behind anointing, I might have been loosing I might have been covered in shame but I am coming from behind, I am coming from being financially behind, this woman made a critical decision if I can touch the hem of His garment: watch this she said I want to touch the hem of His garment which is at the bottom, because that's where I have reached, why would you touch Him at the hem, because that's where I can reach from my way up from the ground; I have to hold on to anything that comes from Him I am tired of loosing, brother even if you sing that boring song I have to grab it cause I am done, if you call for alter call I have to come cause I am done, if you call for bible study I am gonna be there why? Because I am tired of loosing, I am tired of not doing what I was created to do and for all the twelve years she was covered in shame which was characterized by the following

Suffering many afflictions

The case of this woman was very afflicting, the bible doesn't explain how but we can easily ascertain that her condition caused her a terrible heartache. It caused her a lot of discomfort, stress and agony. It was a cause for constant worry and sleepless nights. It is undoubtedly certain that she must have suffered many things associated with her condition, because of the nature of her malady; it was such as could not be made public, without subjecting her to shame, contempt and untold suffering. The shame and the contempt involved pre-occupied her mind all the time especially if her condition was to spill over to the public domain. If your mind is always pre-occupied with shame, as a consequence of your condition, joy and peace will definitely be elusive. You will not enjoy life regardless of how rich or privileged you are in your condition of shame. That person that has little in terms of possessions without any shame to worry about is far better off than you. When you are so engrossed with a hopeless and shameful condition you will go through pain and misery that sometimes, people around you may never know about they may never comprehend what you are grappling with no matter how close they are to you, many times people close to us suffer in silence. This woman suffered alone in obscurity. Shame caused her to suffer in solitary silence, this was her fight, her condition was to shameful to be discussed in the public, she couldn't discuss it with anyone because she definitely knew she would be victimized and ostracized further

Spending all her earnings

It is too costly to try and cover your own shame. I read of people business men, politicians who are on the court corridors every single day trying to clear their names from accusations that are either true or false and they are willing to spend lots of money to try and clear their names from any scandal that is synonymous with shame and the amount of money spent attempting to do so is a lot, this woman must have been wealthy, she visited countless physicians and spent all her earnings hoping to be better, and in the process of trying to erase her shame, she ended up broke, having spent all that she had, her resources were depleted because of shame, she found herself on a spending spree trying to get well but her desperate attempts never yielded any fruit, dealing with shame without Christ is costly this is because shame is like a vampire. It is like a leech that sucks the treasures invested in your life in a subtle way. It cripples your gifting and talents until you cannot operate in them effectively. Regardless of how anointed one is, one cannot minister when they are covered in shame. It will require the blood of Jesus to completely break the power of shame over their life. Only Christ can vindicate and replenish everything that shame has ripped from your life

A deteriorating condition

This woman's health grew worse because the diagnosis wasn't right. No physician seemed to get to the root of her problem, consequently the right prescription was not being administered. She grew weaker and weaker and was now becoming anaemic. This is also true with shame especially when it is not properly addressed. It degenerates into other destructive emotions such as hatred, bitterness, anger, un forgiveness and fear, that have toxic effects on the body, mind and emotions. This is why some people reach a stage where they are un manageable. These destructive emotions drive them over the cliff to a point where they cant stand being in a relationship or marriage. There hearts are so wounded and calloused that they feel nothing for anyone, this woman's condition grew worse even after visiting the physician. But one thing I admire her for, is that she remained optimistic about her healing. She believed she would come out of it someday, despite how bad the situation is, Christ can still heal you and restore your life wholeness

This woman with the issue of blood had to overcome some of these issues that I have listed below issues that breeds shame in order for her to be able to reach up to Jesus as she touched his hem of garment, remember this woman was down, she was in a pit and the bible says she touched the hem of his garment and if you should know the hem of the garment is at the bottom now she reached up many people says she reached down but remember this woman was down so she had to reach up when we understand certain things in our lives that no matter what you find yourself in know that there is a way out of that situation and the reason you in that situation is because God has a purpose: and you should not allow people to determine your value and relevance based on where you are:

1: Rehearsing your past "The woman with the issue of blood made a statement before she reached out to Jesus she said "if I can only touch the hem of his garment I shall be made whole" she obviously forgot about her past she said if I can only touch imagine in order for her to touch the hem of the garment she had to go down: she didn't rehearse her past; and say my whole life I was down so I cant go down again she never rehearsed her past never rehearse your past and be rooted and grounded in the love of God know that whatever you went through in the past if you have repented then God has already forgiven you have to move forward reach out to the hem

2: A vicious cycle of mistakes "the bible says a righteous man may fall seven times but the Lord restores him, have you ever repeated a mistake again and again? Have you ever promised yourself that it wont happen again but somehow, somewhat, it does? Have you ever changed your physical address or your phone number trying to avoid certain people? I remember the first time I fell I promised myself that I will never do that again but then I found myself repeating the same mistake again and again, when you find yourself stuck in repeated mistakes, you feel shameful of yourself, you become ashamed of yourself because you keep doing what you detest when you promise yourself not to do something the bible says she went from doctor to doctor but rather she grew worse but instead of her saying I cant resolve this cycle she reached out to Jesus

3: Low self – esteem "I want you to see that this woman had all the reason to not reach out to Jesus because of her low self – esteem she was covered in shame and it was shameful enough to be a woman in that era and because of her condition she was ostracized from society but she reached out and overcame low self- esteem and Jesus' response after she touched him was "I got you covered"

I got you covered

the most dangerous person is somebody who took a fall but still have his vision

This woman with the issue of blood she had took a fall but even though she was down she had a vision "if only I can touch him" I want to talk to somebody who is reading this book that the fact that you are reading this book means that you are a survivor do you have any idea how many times that enemy tried to kill you this year, do you have any idea how many times he conspired against you, how many time he tried to curse you, how many times he tried to strip the favor of your life? But thank God that what he didn't know is that every morning when you woke up you would put on the armor of God upon your life that's why the enemy cant get you, I refuse to let the enemy beat me because I am covered, God's hand is upon my life, I just want to say to you that don't underestimate the value of what it took for God to cover you, in Genesis 1-3 you notice that Adam and Eve are clothed in glory gear and there is no evidence of any clothing but glory, I don't know if you can handle the reality of glory gears suggest that when I am in His glory I don't need anything else, Adam and Eve are covered in God's glory until they ate the forbidden fruit and then they became aware of what they don't have and they tried to compensate it with fig leaves, people who don't have glory always want to cover them with stuff and they feel like the stuff will compensate the fact that they don't have glory, woe to a church that is so consumed with what they have on than they are oblivious of the presence of Glory that should be on their lives, when you have glory you don't have to hide in trees, when you have glory you don't have to tell people what kind of label clothes you have on, when you have glory on glory on your life you don't try to impress anyone, Joseph was in fact given a multi colored rob by his father that none of his brothers had on when you are anointed by God ladies and gentleman you are in fact shrouded in your own uniqueness you don't have to duplicate or replicate what anybody else is doing but you comfortable in your own skin, comfortable in your own anointing, comfortable in your own gift so Joseph was dressed in a unique coat that no body else had and his brothers threw him in the pit and when they threw him in the pit they did not throw him in the pit without first stripping him of his coat you got to be careful there are people in the church who just want to take your uniqueness, they want to take your dream, they want to take your creativity and will not be satisfied with you falling down if you still have your vision, the most dangerous person is somebody who took a fall but still have his vision, when Joseph got out of the pit he changed clothes and he became dressed in discipline because he is now working for a man called Potiphar and Potiphar's wife develops a crush on Joseph but notice this if you look in the text that no where does it say Joseph doesn't find her attractive, no where does it say this was something that he entertained and even inspite of that he said No, watch this ladies and gentleman Joseph tried to get out of the house, get out of the room he's running for his life, what does Potiphar's wife do? But tear a piece of his robe she tears a piece of his robe why? Because she is trying to snatch his discipline, you got to be careful people will become angry when you tell them No and they will try to find a way to seduce your discipline because they don't understand why you got discipline to say no to what you like, you don't take discipline to say no to something that you are not attracted to but to walk away from something you can have and say I would rather have God than have this the enemy is doing all he can to pull your clothes of discipline because he cannot understand why you got strong and the reason I got strong is I have been through a lot and God is covering me He has clothed me with redemption threads the prodigal son had these clothes, redemption threads when he left because when he left home he asked for his inheritance early he spent all he had in riotous living and he woke up in a pig pen with pig dirt all over his robe and the bible declares that he came to himself and said I am going back to my father's house now watch this! He is going back to his father's house with stains and with mud and with alcohol stains but his father said I am not going to keep you in that because where I am getting ready to take you I do not want you to show the stains from your past, I am getting ready to dress you up again so that people wont even know the kind of mistakes you made, I am giving you a new life. Some of you have to give God the praise for taking the stains of your clothes, people don't even understand the kind of life that I lived but God's grace dressed me up for my future. Jesus told a parable of a man who goes from Jerusalem to Jericho and the problem is he was going down, he is going down from Jerusalem to Jericho, it is never the intention or the mind of God for you to go down it is God's intention for you to be increased, elevated and blessed some of you might be reading and saying but I am done right now thank God you are down because now we can curse everything in your life that is holding you down the devil is a liar God will cover you, I don't know where some of you are but some of you have to be excited knowing that where you are is the lowest that you will ever going to be because if you can live to see 2014 it's a sign that I am going to make it the man was moving from Jerusalem to Jericho watch this! And he falls amongst thieves and the first thing the thieves did is thy stripped him why did they strip him? They were trying to get the glory gear of him, they were trying to get the discipline of him, they were trying to get the uniqueness of him, they were trying to get the vision of him, they were trying to get redemption of him, I want you to notice this they did not beat him until they stripped him the enemy cant touch you as long as you got on glory but the moment you take of your glory that when the enemy can touch you, some of you have to shout cause the enemy thought he was going to kill you this year but he didn't know that you had glory on you if you didn't have glory on do you know how many people were trying to kill you? Do you know how many people were wishing you bad but they didn't know that every morning when you woke up you would put on the whole armor of God that's why cancer cannot beat you, poverty cannot beat you, because God's favor is upon my life, God's glory is upon my life that's why I refuse to give in, I don't have a lot of money, I don't have a lot friends but the glory is on me, I thank God that He dressed me in His glory the bible says the man fall among thieves and they stripped him of his glory they beat him down and the text says he was half dead and the lawyer passes by and not only does a lawyer pass by but a priest passed by, this man is half dead and he was not even asking them to give him money all he wanted was to be covered, this is the problem with the church when someone is down and half dead all they need is to be covered, not to talk about him, not to walk by and leave them, I want you to know whatever you are going through know that God has got you covered and here comes a good Samaritan and sees him by the side of the road and none of the church people would cover him he was not even in the church but he had a heart its amazing that sometimes non-church people will be nicer to you that those who claim to be born again spirit filled and walking with the Holy ghost the Samaritan sees him by the side of the road, limping, broken, bruised, hurting, crying, naked and then the Samaritan bring out oil and wine and poured it on the man open sores now watch this! The oil soothed the wound, the wine made it burn ladies and gentleman the reason you feel like your life is burning is that sometimes when God is healing you sometimes it feels good but there are some other time when it hurts and we sit and say God why are you doing this to me? And He says just sit and wait its part of your healing process its hurting you but its healing you and the good Samaritan puts him on the donkey and puts him in the inn, praise God no matter where you are He got you covered

CHAPTER SIX

The way out of shame

....the only way out of shame is in Him

Psalms 34:5-6 "they looked to Him and were radiant, and their faces were not ashamed 6; this poor man cried out, and the Lord heard him, and saved him out of all his troubles

In John 8 we read a phenomenal story of a woman who was caught in the act of Adultery and it's so amazing, do you ever wonder why the bible says "she was caught in the act?" the fact that she was caught in the act means the people who had witnessed it where right there, it's one thing when people who take you to Jesus heard about it from other people and it's another thing for the ones who caught you are present, she couldn't defend herself because she was caught in the act, you can defend yourself if there are no witnesses but she couldn't defend herself, I find it very interesting in my story of shame that even though the people affected by my actions were there and some of the things that were brought as an accusation to me were not true I didn't defend myself in all. I really want us to take a deep look into this story the bible says Jesus is busy teaching in the temple imagine in our time a pastor is teaching during our Sunday services and obviously there's order in the church and everyone is silence as they are concentrating on the word of God that is being brought by the Pastor imagine they start hearing what seemed like someone screaming and the noise gets louder and louder to a point where the voice of the pastor is not heard (every time we lose the voice of the shepherd we lose the ability to follow and when we don't follow then we left vulnerable)but this time it's not just a voice that's screaming but voices a great commotion people are screaming, shouting, cursing, stone her, stone her, others are crying because the person who is about to be stoned is their mother now can you imagine the church people shifting their concentration so as to hear the noise coming out of the temple but drawing in (there's a voice outside the temple drawing in and if you pay attention to it; that voice will draw you out) (it's so important brethren as a child of God that you should never take your concentration out from the church and focus it outside the church because the voice that comes from outside are voices that shouts "stone her that's all you will ever hear from the outside, stone her, an adulterer, she thought she is perfect, she thought she had it all, but now look, stone her these are the voices that come out of the temple we should always concentrate on the voice that comes from the church not necessary, from the Pastor off course we should listen to the Pastor but I am talking about the voice within the Voice the true voice, the way, the life and the savior that's Jesus and you can never go wrong on that voice as we continue with the story you will see why we have to follow that voice, now suddenly as they were all paying attention to the outside voices the doors of the temple swings wide open as the crowd comes in (imagine when you concentrate on the outside voices,(the voices that tell you that you not good enough, you can never make it, you must be stoned etc) the doors will open and you will not go through them what you will see is other people coming through while you sitting there, there is no recording in this story that people went out, until Jesus said "if any of you don't have sin be the first to stone her and they went away one by one that's the only time people went out when Jesus said so, crowds pressed in the temple to see what was gonna happen to the poor woman some were holding their mouths in shock, some were holding stones ready to stone her and the one thing that all the church people caught their attention was the naked woman and she had her hand on her private parts as she stumbled in and all the church people moved away in shock leaving her alone before Jesus (that should be our attitude as children of God when one of us is naked yes we should be shocked but we should move away giving space for them to be before Jesus) in her mind she was feeling shame, but in reality that's the best place to be alone naked before Jesus because when He covers you no one can uncover you. And that was the best place for her to be and the last time a human being discovered their nakedness they blamed it on someone but this woman as naked as she was she never blamed anyone, she had no one she was using as her covering she stood naked and you can imagine the shame that she was experiencing firstly the whole community knew about her story, her family, her friends even her relatives her story was out in the public, its one thing when your story is private, but its another thing when your story is public, I can imagine the family of the man she slept with how angry they were, her family and friends everyone was angry and affected, people that looked up to her were disappointed in her it was shame that she was experiencing, she was literally covered in Shame and she is in the centre surrounded by people ready to stone her and the accuser's voices shouted saying unto Jesus John 8:4 they said unto Jesus, master this woman was taken in adultery, in the very act, 5: now Moses in the law commanded us that such should be stoned: but what do you say? Now I can see the woman looking attentively to Jesus because her life was depending on what He was going to say, (that's why its so important for us to look to Jesus because our lives are depended on what He has to say) and Jesus kept queit for a while and stooped on the ground, I believe the reason why He stooped down was (even though she thought Jesus was quiet on her in his quietness He was passing a message to her as He stooped on the ground He was passing a message to the woman as He stooped on the dirt, saying when you can't get to me, when you find yourself in a moment of shame, in a moment of weakness I don't mind getting down in the dirt for you and the woman did not understand what He meant by being quiet and stooping on the ground and Jesus stooped for the second time saying I don't care how many times I have to get down for you I will keep getting down for you and if Jesus could get his hands dirty who are we to judge so when they continued to ask Him, He lifted up himself, and said unto them, He that is without sin among you, let him first cast a stone at her, and there was a noise of stones being thrown on the ground as the people started leaving one by one and Jesus was left alone with the woman standing before her and Jesus said one of the most powerful words He said "Woman" the question is how could he call her that when others were calling her an Adulterer, calling her all kinds of names and Jesus comes and calls her Woman even in the very act of being an Adulterer He calls her woman, and he asked her a confusing and difficult question he said "is there anyone left to accuse you" even though all the accusers were gone but there was one person left and she didn't know whether Jesus would accuse her or not but as she battled in her mind what to say she found herself saying "No one Lord" and Jesus knowing her heart said "even though you thought I may accuse you but my answer is "Neither do I condemn you, go and sin no more" what a powerful statement so when Jesus said go and sin no more he was setting her free from all those outside the temple affected by her actions here are some of the practical ways to overcome shame the first thing you have to do is you need to stop thinking about your past failures. Are you ignoring them? No! you are ignoring a lie, not the sin, because the sin has been dealt with and washed away. Therefore, you are meditating on something that no longer exist! If your sins are in the depths of the sea, then why are you still thinking about them? Micah 7:19 "he will have compassion upon us; he will subdue our iniquities; and thou will cast all their sins into the depths of the sea" you need to stop focusing on the problem (which has been dealt with), and begin to praise God for the solution to the problem, and think about how you have been washed clean from those failures! Instead of meditating on a lie, begin to meditate on the truth in God's word concerning your past failures and here are some great verses to get you started Isaiah 1:18, 1 John 1:9, Psalms 103:12, Titus 2:14, Ephesians 1: 7, Romans 8:1 and the second thing you have to do is disassociate yourself from your past! Why do you think God wanted us to be new creations? Because He did not want your past to be part of you anymore! 2 Corinthians 5:17 "Therefore if any man be in Christ, he is a new creature: old things are passed away: behold, all things are become new" now that our past failures has been forgiven, we need to leave them there and press forward towards the things God has for us: Philippians 3:13 "this one thing I do, forgetting those things which are behind, and reaching forth unto those things which are before"

CHAPTER SEVEN

Dealing with Shame

...if I can only touch the hem of his garment I shall be well

When I was going through shame I was complaining, blaming certain people for being the cause of my shame, angry with them and these were the words that Dolly the woman that I love and the one who stood with me in times of difficulty said "everything that's happening to you Marshall has nothing to do with any person but you" I never understood what she was saying why would she say such and yet she knows that the reason I was experiencing the shame is because someone exposed me and these words got stuck on me cause we have a tendency like I had of blaming other people as the reason why certain things happened in our lives, Adam blamed Eve and till this day someone somewhere is blaming someone the issue here is not what someone did or didn't do but the issue is I,

"If I can only touch the hem of his garment I shall be well"

Dolly's words really ministered to me because I was blaming people for my shame I really wanted someone to transfer my hate to, so that I could stop hating myself. And the terror of being judged was my fear how was I going to face the brethren? So if I could transfer my shame on someone then I would be free from judgment people would stop focusing on me and focus on the one that I shift my shame to or if I couldn't shift my shame on anyone then I would just run away, I wanted to run away from my shame that is running away from church but what Dolly said changed my life for good she said Marshall running away from church won't do you good this is what I want you to do for me go back to church and face everyone that you ashamed to face you should set an example by doing what is good. If you live openly and honestly, you set an example of virtue, humanness, restoration, and healing. You give others permission to join you on your journey despite the fear of being judged and rejection it might elicit when they know that they are not alone in their experience and she went on to say that more of us who amass the courage to embark openly on this path, the more normal this experience becomes, effectively eliminating the tactic of shame and isolation that the enemy so often uses to cause us to falter she continued saying the world needs people who have survived mistakes, tragedies, and trials to help the rest of us through. The world needs you to let go of self – pity and shame regarding your life experiences, too. The world needs you to use the things you have learned for good, stop letting your past mistakes define you and affect your value, let go of separation and victimhood and find meaning in what you have been through not running away from the church and she went on to say running away from church is not the solution you actually not running away from people but you running away from yourself and that moved me and brought understanding to know that he first thing to do when dealing with shame is to eliminate any other persons what they did or what they did not do, and secondly you have to eliminate focusing on yourself in other words blaming yourself for what happened to you cause I started focusing on how weak I was and an embarrassment and that I might not be called of God because if I was really was called then such thing will have never happened but that's a lie from the enemy, you have to know that whatever is happening around me or to me is not because of other people's actions but you have to understand that God is dealing with me most of the times we blame our enemies and we wish our enemies bad but we fail to understand and know that just as God has good plans for you He also has good plans for our enemies. The bible tells us a story about the woman who had an issue of blood for twelve years and she went to doctors but she was no better I want you to imagine what she had to go through

But this woman never focused on what she had lost and how she had lost it, she never focused on what she was experiencing, she never focused on any other person or that the doctors had failed her, or that the reason she was like that was because of someone she said this problem I have is not about anyone but its about me therefore If I, not them I can only touch the hem of His garment then I shall be well there is something that really moved me in this story, the bible says she touched the hem of his garment and if you would know the hem of the garment is at the bottom so in order for her to reach out to the hem she had to go down, she never touched the face of Jesus but the hem in other words she knew she was down and loosing blood so she decided to touch anything closest to her since she was down anything closest that's coming from Him

The prodigal son did not focus on anything but him, he said I will arise and go back to my father he never blamed anyone he made changes

When the axe head fell into the water he never made excuses and say it's the axe manufacturing company that don't know how to make axes anyone, he didn't say it was so and so he made changes he was willing to go to the man of God and ask for help: the axe head represents God's power it's not our power it's His all we are is good stewards of that power we don't make excuses we make changes, *"you can't give up shame without giving up pride" Shame is nothing more than denial of the truth" and the absence of truth you can't defeat the devil*

Dealing with shame you have to be proud of who you are, and not ashamed of how someone else sees you, you have to tell the truth and shame the devil

Here are some few steps to move through shame

Ground yourself in the present

In other words, start where you are. Until you fully accept where you are you cant move forward. Get real with yourself, this is the time to fully sit with the reality of the present moment and allow yourself to feel any and all the feelings that come up for you, often our stuckness happens because we are trying to avoid these feelings, so its important to just let yourself feel them. Remember they are not wrong they just are what they are. When you feel them, you can get them up and out, which leaves you with a greater sense of determination and clarity

Shame is like running out of wine, running out of that which was sweet and everybody enjoyed you then suddenly the wine ran out and shame kicks in, but Jesus will fill you up he will fill that emptiness only if you cooperate with Him in the time of emptiness, and do what He tells you to do, you have to allow him to cleanse you first with the washing of the water of the word and fill your vessel then when you recover whatever you draw out is the best is better than the first

CHAPTER EIGHT

No Condemnation

"There is therefore now no condemnation to them
which are in Christ Jesus, who walk not after the flesh,
but after the Spirit" Romans 8:1

In Romans 8:1 the bible says there is therefore now no condemnation to them which are in Christ Jesus, who walk not after the flesh, but after the Spirit" it doesn't matter what you have done God does not hold your past failures He has forgiven you and forgotten about it its only one person who keeps reminding us of our past failures the enemy the accuser of the brethren the one that condemns the bible says in John 3:17 "for God did not sent His son into the world to condemn the world; but that the world through him might be saved" so Jesus's purpose is to save the world to save those who feel condemned or who are condemned and not to condemn them its so amazing when you read the story of the woman who was caught in the act of adultery the truth was this woman was an adulterer that is why they wanted to stone her because of what she had done and they called her an adulterer but Jesus the one who had the right to condemn her what did he do? He called her woman instead of calling her an adulterer he called her woman he said to her neither will I condemn you go and sin no more He didn't condemn her

CHAPTER NINE

It's not what you lost it's what you have left

"and they which heard it, being convicted by their own conscience went out one by one, beginning with the eldest, even unto the last: and Jesus was left alone; and the woman standing in the midst" John 8:9

I want you to imagine what this woman actually had lost this woman being a member of the community and I am sure respected on a certain of who she was and all that we not told whether she had children or not but we all are sure that somehow she had close family and was regarded as a human being in the society and after being caught obviously the news went around the community everybody went out to see her as she was being dragged to the temple by the Pharisees so this woman actually had lost respect from all the other woman and even from the children because while she was being dragged they were watching and I am sure they were also shouting and scolding her just like what the society does after someone has been caught doing the wrong things so she had lost respect form all people and she also had lost her reputation if she had a name they no longer called her by her name she had a new name she was called the woman caught in the act of adultery she was an adulterer now have you ever lost your reputation? And people no longer see you as that worshipper or see you as that great man of God because of something you did this is exactly where she was she had lost her reputation and also she had lost her dignity imagine being dragged half naked before all people and worse you being dragged to the temple all the other Christians see your nakedness she had lost her dignity and she also lost her confidence I would have she also lost her pride she was humiliated in front of the whole community, she lost relationships I am sure if she had a husband that man was ready to divorce her, she lost trust people never trusted her again, she lost her covering now she was naked, she lost her accountability, this woman had lost everything after being divorced she was going to be in the streets cause no one would want to associate with her, she had lost her future literally now what excites and encourages me in this sad story is what I want to encourage you no matter where you are, what you have lost in your life, some of you might have lost your husband, your husband left you and not only did he leave you but he also took everything away from you, some of you lost your job, you lost everything in your life but I am here to say to you its not what you lost that matters its what you have left this woman after all that she had lost the bible says after all people were gone she was standing alone with Jesus and that's all you need, yes you have lost all, but what do you have left? She had Jesus left with her and that's all you need let them take away everything from you but as long as you have Jesus you have all you need because Jesus will cover your nakedness what people have stripped away from you Jesus will cover you watch what happens after everyone was gone out of the temple now I am sure they were waiting for her outside because they wanted revenge the family of the man she slept with I am sure they were angry with her they wanted to show her their piece of mind so it was not over even though she was safe with Jesus but she still had to go home and face those people this is what blew my mind in this story the bible says after all had gone and she was left alone standing with Jesus, Jesus said a powerful statement to her he said "go and sin no more" what that means is Jesus was setting her free not only from herself but also from the people who were waiting for her outside "go" that's what Jesus said to her in other words she was naked before Jesus and Jesus covered her nakedness and sends her home again Jesus wants to cover your nakedness whatever you have lost he wants to restore your dignity again, he wants to restore your reputation again, he wants to restore your confidence again, he wants to restore your sense of security again, he wants to restore you materially again, he wants to restore your reputation again, he wants to restore you so that you can function again without holding back from what has happened in the past the past has been dealt with its not what you have lost its what you have left. In the book of Amos 3:12 theirs is a very interesting story the bible says "thus saith the Lord; as the shepherd taketh out of the mouth of the lion two legs, or a piece of an ear; so shall the children of Israel be taken out that dwell in Samaria in the corner of a bed, and in Damascus in a couch" this story is mind blowing a shepherd comes and sees a lion a devouring a lame and the lame has already been eaten if I was a shepherd I would have just accepted that I have lost one sheep but what does he do he opens the mouth of the lion risking his life and takes out two legs and a piece of ear, now what that means is its not what you have lost its what you have left the lame was eaten but there was something left even though all was lost but there was something redeemable that was two legs and a piece of ear now that means even though you have lost all but if you still have legs to stand on what you have heard God saying about your life then God can still redeem you it doesn't matter what you lost it doesn't matter the pain you feeling as a matter of fact your pain has purpose there's a reason why you in pain and the pain is not over what you lost its about what you are about to gain and the reason the devil cant stand you is because he sees a preview of your coming attraction its not what I have lost but its about what I am about to gain so you must make sure you still standing on the promises of God because its not what you lost but its what you have left

CHAPTER TEN

The come back anointing

"Came behind him, and touched the border of his garment: and immediately her issue of blood stopped" Luke 8:44

Luke 8:44 says **she came from behind** and touched Jesus. God wants me to tell you that: she came from behind: to tell those who have been fighting, through depression, shame, through suffering and loosing that if you begin to worship me it's the beginning of a season in your life where you **come from behind** I am getting ready to turn the tables over, the anointing upon your life is a come from behind anointing, I might have been loosing I might have been covered in shame but I am coming from behind, I am coming from being financially behind, this woman made a critical decision if I can touch the hem of His garment: watch this she said I want to touch the hem of His garment which is at the bottom, because that's where I have reached, why would you touch Him at the hem, because that's where I can reach from my way up from the ground; I have to hold on to anything that comes from Him I am tired of loosing, brother even if you sing that boring song I have to grab it cause I am done, if you call for alter call I have to come cause I am done, if you call for bible study I am going be there why? Because I am tired of loosing, I am tired of not doing what I am called to do I wrote this chapter to encourage people that there is a come back anointing God will restore you more than what you lost, you can come back more will welcome you than those that rejected you, I want to challenge someone to rise up, Jepthah in the book of Judges came from behind he was in the land of Tob and the elders sent people to get him back, I don't know where you are right now in your life but if you can reach out to God He will bring you out from the place you are the bible says we are not the tail but we are the head its your season to come from behind

CHAPTER ELEVEN

What the bible says about shame

"if we confess our sins, he is faithful and just to forgive us our
sins and to cleanse us from all unrighteousness" 1 John 1:9

"No temptation has overtaken you that is not common to man.
God is faithful, and he will not let you be tempted beyond your
ability, but with the temptation he will also provide the way of
escape, that you may be able to endure it" 1 Corinthians 10:13

"Repent, therefore, of this wickedness of yours, and pray to the Lord
that, if possible, the intent of your heart may be forgiven you" Acts 8:22

"My little children, I am writing these things to you so that
you may not sin. But if anyone does sin, we have an advocate
with the father, Jesus Christ the righteous" 1 John 2:1

"For everyone who calls on the name of the
Lord will be saved" Romans 10:13

"He will wipe away every tear from their eyes, and death shall be
no more, neither shall there be mourning, nor crying, nor pain
anymore, for the former things have passed away" Revelation 21:4

"For all have sinned and fall short of the glory of God" Romans 3:23

"Repent therefore, and turn again, that your
sins may be blotted out" Acts 3:19

"He will again have compassion on us; he will tread our iniquities
underfoot. You will cast all our sins into the depths of the sea" Micah 7:19

"For God so loved the world that He gave His only son, that whoever
believes in him should not perish but have eternal life" John 3:16

"For God did not send his son into the world to condemn the world,
but in order that the world might be saved through him" John 3:17

"Flee from sexual immorality. Every other sin a person
commits is outside the body, but the sexually immoral
person sins against his own body" 1 Corinthians 6:18

"Beloved, do not believe every spirit, but test the spirits
to see whether they are from God, for many false
prophets have gone out into the world" 1 John 4:1

"Because, if you confess with your mouth that Jesus
is Lord and believe in your heart that God raised him
from the dead, you will be saved" Romans 10:9

"the Lord is not slow to fulfill his promise as some count
slowness, but is patient toward you, not wishing that any should
perish, but that all should reach repentance" 2 Peter 3:9

"And Peter said to them, repent and be baptized every one of
you in the name of Jesus Christ for the forgiveness of your sins,
and you will receive the gift of the Holy spirit" Acts 2:38

"He is the propitiation for our sins, and not for ours only
but also for the sins of the whole world" 1 John 2:2

"Fear not, for you will not be ashamed; be not confounded, for you will not be disgraced; for you will forget the shame of your youth, and the reproach of your widowhood you will remember no more" Isaiah 54:4

"For the Lord disciplines the one he loves, and chastises every son whom he receives" Hebrews 12:6

"Who desires all people to be saved and to come to the knowledge of the truth" 1 Timothy 2:4

"Whoever believes in him is not condemned, but whoever does not believe is condemned already, because he has not believed in the name of the only son of God" John 3:18

"Behold, I stand at the door and knock, if anyone hears my voice and opens the door, I will come in to him and eat with him, and he with me" Revelation 3:20

Printed in the United States
By Bookmasters